THE CAREER RESOURCE LIBRARY

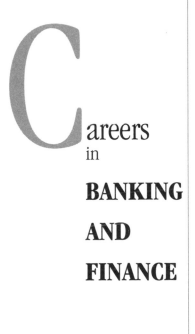

areers
in
BANKING
AND
FINANCE

Patricia Haddock

The Rosen Publishing Group, Inc.
NEW YORK

Published in 1990, 1998, 2001 by The Rosen Publishing Group, Inc.
29 East 21st Street, New York, NY 10010

Revised Edition 2001

Cover © Stewart Cohen/Indexstock

Library of Congress Cataloging-in-Publication Data

Haddock, Patricia.
Careers in banking and finance/by Patricia Haddock.
p. cm.
Includes bibliographical references.
Summary: Describes the various jobs available in banking and finance and the education and training required.
ISBN 0-8239-3446-2
1. Banks and banking—Vocational guidance—United States—Juvenile literature. 2. Financial services industry—Vocational guidance—United States—Juvenile literature. [1. Banks and banking—Vocational guidance. 2. Financial services industry—Vocational guidance. 3. Vocational guidance.] I. Title.
HG1609.1133 1989
332.1'023'73—dc20
                                                    89-37693
                                                         CIP
                                                          AC

Manufactured in the United States of America

Contents

	Introduction	1
1.	Banking: Changes and Challenges	4
2.	Finance: The World of Wall Street	19
3.	Choosing the Right Job in Banking and Finance	28
4.	Insider Information	88
5.	Getting the Job You Want	92
	Glossary	110
	For More Information	124
	For Further Reading	128
	Index	131

Introduction

Today you can turn on your computer and pay your bills, find out your checking account balance, or apply for a loan. You can buy and sell stocks online while eating breakfast, or exchange American dollars for foreign currency without ever leaving home. You can buy everything from stamps to movie tickets at the nearest ATM—but only after having your eye scanned by a laser that can identify you by the pattern of blood vessels in your retina.

It may sound like science fiction, but it's not. Chances are that your own local bank offers most, if not all, of these services right now. New technologies like these are changing the way financial companies do business. Customers are now able to perform many of the functions that before were completed only by bank tellers and brokers. This has changed many jobs in the field of banking and finance.

We are in the midst of a revolution in financial services. Banks of the future will look quite different—and perform different functions—than banks today. In part this is due to the availability of advanced technology, and in part because banks and brokerages now offer similar services.

Until recently, banks and brokerages were different types of businesses. Each offered unique services and products. Banks offered checking and savings accounts and made loans, while brokerages sold stocks and bonds. A person worked in banking or in a brokerage and rarely moved from one to the other. The two worlds were highly regulated by federal and state laws, and there was not much competition between banking and finance.

Then, in the early 1980s, the government began to remove many of the regulations that had previously separated banking and finance. With deregulation came competition. Suddenly, banks and brokerages were competing for the same customers and offering similar products and services. Large banks began to buy smaller banks. Companies began to pour money into new technology in order to keep up with the competition and position themselves on the cutting edge of the financial world. What was once a rather staid profession became a high-powered and highly competitive industry.

Deregulation has also opened the door to opportunity. Once careers in banking and finance followed pretty straight lines. That is no longer true. Today, banking and finance are not really two different worlds. Some jobs are still unique to one; for instance, brokerage houses do not have tellers. However, in most areas, banks and financial services companies offer similar services and products. Careers in one are the same as careers in the other, or very similar. For instance, both industries need research analysts, so those skills can be transferred from a bank to a brokerage and vice versa. The opportunity for crossover in the two fields increases the number of jobs available for qualified people.

The jobs in this book are described in broad terms. Although there are common jobs in banking and finance, their duties, their importance within a company, and the career opportunities they offer vary from corporation to corporation.

This book gives you broad ideas about the jobs available. You must talk to different companies to determine where your personality will fit best, how the jobs you are interested in are staffed, how employees are trained, and how far and where you can go within the company. The chapter titled Choosing the Right Job in Banking and Finance and the For More Information section will help you find that out.

Banking: Changes and Challenges

"Once banking and finance were two separate parts of the business. This isn't the best way to serve clients. Over the past ten years, the industry has been consolidating, and banking and financial services have been combined. Many banks have partnered with, and acquired, financial services businesses. The distinction seems seamless now. Today, we are total wealth managers, helping clients manage both assets and liabilities. It takes hard work and study to succeed, but it's worth the effort. This is an exciting industry."

—David Skolnik, senior vice president and director of national sales and marketing for private client services, Wells Fargo Bank

In the past, being a banker meant processing savings and checking deposits and withdrawals from customers' accounts, lending money to businesses and individuals, and making sure all the money balanced at the end of the day. Sometimes you opened a safe deposit box for someone. People believed that bankers ran their businesses according to the Rule of 3-6-3: Pay 3 percent on deposits; charge 6 percent on loans; get to the golf course by 3:00 PM.

No one believes that anymore. Banking has changed, and changed drastically.

Banking today is one of the most competitive and exciting industries in the world. Banks compete not only with all other banks, but with nonbank companies such as Merrill Lynch, Fidelity Investments, and Charles Schwab.

Once upon a time, banks could count on keeping their customers forever. They can no longer do that. Customer loyalty to one bank is largely a thing of the past. Customers look for the best return on their money, convenience, and a variety of products that meet their financial needs.

Demanding customers, deregulation of the banking industry, and competition, not only from banks but also other financial and nonfinancial industries, have all contributed to the changing world of banking. To survive and thrive, banks must meet their competition head-on. And that means that opportunities exist for sharp, eager, ambitious young people who want to participate in the world of money and finance.

A Short History of Banking

Banks and bankers have been around for thousands of years, but modern banking dates only from the sixteenth century, when Italian bankers conducted their business from benches. The word "bank" comes from the Italian word for bench, *banca*.

In England, goldsmiths took on the role of bankers. Wealthy people, usually merchants, stored their gold and silver in a goldsmith's vault. The goldsmith, in turn, gave the owners receipts for the gold, and the merchants used their receipts to get credit. The receipts proved that they could pay for the merchandise they ordered.

The goldsmiths soon discovered that they could lend the gold and silver they stored for the merchants and charge interest to the people who borrowed it. They could also attract more merchants to deposit gold and silver with them by paying interest to depositors. The English goldsmiths became bankers.

Early in America's history, banks often issued their own money. If you lived on a farm near Lincoln, Nebraska, essentially, you paid your bills with money issued by your local Lincoln bank. People living in New Orleans used money issued by a New Orleans bank. Almost as many currencies were in circulation as there were banks. It was very confusing, especially if you traveled. It was also dangerous.

If one of the banks failed, depositors lost the money they had on deposit with that bank. All the money the bank had issued was also lost. It was totally worthless!

The U.S. government decided that something had to be done to safeguard the value of money, and Congress passed the National Bank Acts of 1863 and 1864 to create a trustworthy paper currency. The worth of the money depended on the federal government, not individual banks.

Early banks offered little in the way of careers. They were much smaller than today's banks, and usually had only two employees: the president and a clerk. The president acted as cashier, making loans and running the business. The clerk acted as teller and bookkeeper. Most of the transactions they handled were cash, but checks became popular after the Civil War. Soon after, banks started making real estate and personal loans.

Then, in 1929, the stock market crashed. Many banks suffered overwhelming losses from which they could not recover. Banks closed, unable to give people back the money they had on deposit. This was the worst stock market crash in the history of the United States.

Some people lost their entire life savings in one day. Many of the bank failures were caused because bankers had used bank money to make various investments in the stock market. Some of those investments were very risky. When the market crashed, the banks failed.

In order to prevent a recurrence of this kind of financial catastrophe, the United States Congress decided to separate commercial banks, which take deposits, from investment banks, which underwrite corporate securities. That means that the bank buys an issue of bonds or stock from a company and then sells the securities to investors. Commercial banks and investment banks have been separate ever since. This separation and other tight government regulations characterized banking for the next fifty years.

In 1933, Congress passed the Glass-Steagall Act, one of the most significant laws governing banking. This and other legislation placed severe restrictions on what banks could and could not do. For instance, banks could offer only certain products and types of loans. Legislation also governed how much interest a bank could pay on deposits or charge on loans. What one bank offered was pretty much the same as what every other bank offered. There was little competition, and each bank did business pretty much the same as all other banks.

Deregulation

Until a few years ago, careers in banking were fairly straightforward. You worked in bank operations or in lending, and that was it.

Then, in the early 1980s, banks were deregulated. Banks and banking careers will never be the same again.

Until very recently, commercial banks made money on the "spread"—the difference between the interest a bank paid to borrow money and what it charged people who borrowed money from it.

For instance, a bank might pay 4 percent to borrow the money it lent to a home buyer at 8 percent. The 4 percent spread, or difference between what the bank paid for the money and what it charged the customer to borrow it, was the bank's profit.

During the days of heavy government regulation, banks made good profits on the spread.

In the early 1980s, however, the interest banks paid to borrow money rose much higher than what they were earning on old mortgages and loans. Profits tumbled.

Other kinds of financial service businesses that were not regulated, such as money-market mutual funds, began paying investors 14 percent or more on their money. By law, banks could pay only 5 1/2 to 5 3/4 percent.

What would you do if you were a bank customer and you could get 10 percent more on your money someplace else? That's right: Take your money out of the bank and move it elsewhere. And that is exactly what many depositors did. Money poured out of banks and into other investments.

Consumers put their money in money-market mutual funds or interest-bearing checking accounts. Corporate money managers found new ways of financing loans for their companies that were more cost-effective. Suddenly banks began losing deposits, and some banks once again began to fail. This time, deposits were insured by the federal government, however, so depositors did not lose their money. Again, Congress had to act.

Banks needed a way of competing with industries that were not subject to the same regulations as they were. But changing the regulations would take time. Meanwhile, banks had to conserve profits or minimize the effects of the losses they were suffering. They started closing branches and cutting staff.

Eventually, Congress phased out many of the old regulations so that banks could better compete with nonbank competitors. In 1982, with the passage of the Garn-St. Germain Depository Institutions Act, banks could begin offering services similar to those of their nonbank competitors.

Today, banks offer so many services that it would take an entire book to describe them. Computers and advances in electronics have revolutionized banking and led to the creation of new, innovative products and services such as ATMs, online banking, and smart cards.

New Products and Services

Banks grow by becoming more profitable. They do that by marketing their products and services and by expanding in certain areas of the marketplace that they have chosen as their own. Banks began to better define their markets and to market to specific audiences; that is, they identified the products they wanted to sell and the people and organizations that might want to buy those products.

For example, if you decide to start a dog-walking business, you have to market your service. You do that by identifying who you want for customers. Do you want to walk large dogs or small dogs? Then you have to identify how you can reach people who own the kinds of dogs you want to walk. And you have to convince them you are the best dog-walker they can find.

The process is much more complicated for large businesses that have competitors on every corner.

Banks began to search for new products to offer customers, such as foreign exchange trading and home banking. Many banks began to offer discount brokerage services that enable customers to buy and sell securities without using a broker.

Some banks offer so many products that employees must specialize in specific areas. A customer can open a checking account, make a deposit in a savings account, buy and sell stocks, and invest in an individual retirement account, all under one roof. All of these specialty areas help to create jobs.

The Future of Banking

Over the last few years, banks have begun to invest in new technologies with names like super-ATMs, smart cards, and electronic banking. Technology will also significantly affect future employment as banks hire people who can help them maximize the opportunities offered to them by the Internet. The technology they are developing is designed to make banking easier and faster for everyone involved.

For instance, in banks around the world, automated teller machines print out instant bank statements, make change, and dispense a wide variety of items, ranging from movie tickets to traveler's checks to stamps. According to the American Bankers Association, at the end of 1999, there were 227,000 ATMs processing 11 billion transactions in the United States alone.

Most high-tech ATMs have two-way phones that let customers talk to bank officers in a remote, centralized location. Customers at the ATM can fill out a loan or credit card application on the ATM's touch-sensitive keyboard. If they have any questions, help is just a phone call away.

A California company is designing an ATM that will let travelers exchange currency at 35,000 feet. These ATMs will be installed on airplanes. BankAtlantic in Florida has ATMs on twenty-seven cruise ships.

Smart cards—also known as digicash or electronic cash cards—are another new invention. A smart card is a small plastic card with a microprocessor computer chip embedded inside it. The cards store the electronic equivalent of cash. For instance, say that you want to buy a candy bar. Instead of paying with cash, you swipe your card over a special terminal at the store counter. The money is automatically deducted from your card. Running out of money on your card? Just take it to the nearest ATM and transfer cash from your checking or savings account to your smart card. No money in your account? Borrow some cash from a friend by transferring it from his or her card to yours. Transfers can also be done by phone or over the Internet.

Smart cards work somewhat like credit cards, but without the costly online verification process that credit cards require. This makes smart cards much cheaper to use.

One of the most exciting areas in banking right now is electronic banking. Electronic banking allows customers to take care of many of their banking needs by computer. Customers with a modem can bank online. They can check account balances, pay bills, invest in various savings plans, transfer money between accounts, or download bank and credit card statements.

Another recent trend in banking is the use of debit cards. Like a check, a point-of-sale (POS) debit card draws money directly from your checking account. For banks, debit cards mean less paperwork and fewer bounced checks. They speed up processing time, because the money is deducted immediately from your checking account. For banks, debit cards are a major step toward paperless banking. A debit card also has advantages for consumers. You don't acquire debt as with a credit card. Many people find debit cards to be convenient, and they like the way that the cards don't cause them as many added fees. There are also no interest charges. Debit cards can make it easier to manage your money. Approximately 300 million debit card transactions are processed each month. According to Bankrate.com, an online publication for consumers, U.S. banks make approximately $1.9 billion a year in ATM surcharges with an average of 950 million ATM transactions processed each month.

What advantages do new technologies offer? An interest transaction costs about one cent versus twenty-seven cents for an ATM transaction, and $1.07 for a transaction with a full-service teller. Moving money electronically is much cheaper and faster than moving money by hand.

Electronic banking is efficient for customers, too. Instead of standing in line at their local branches, customers can access their accounts whenever they want without leaving home. The end result is like having a personal bank branch right inside the customer's computer.

Another advantage comes from helping customers feel more in control of their money. By allowing them to take a more hands-on role in their banking, banks keep customers happy. And keeping customers happy, in these competitive times, is necessary for every bank's survival. According to the Department of Labor (DOL), employment in the banking industry is expected to increase at a much slower rate than the economy as a whole. In fact, the DOL predicts practically no growth for large banks and slightly increased growth for credit unions and regional banks. Mergers among banks are expected to continue, and this will also slow employment growth as banks consolidate staffs.

Declines in the employment of tellers and clerical employees will continue as the use of ATMs and electronic banking grows. Generally, banks will look for people with marketing, sales, and financial experience. However, the DOL predicts that employment of securities and financial services sales representatives in the banking industry will double in the next ten years.

More computer specialists will be needed as banks develop new technologies and maximize existing ones. This will increase the need for customer service representatives as banks create and staff centralized call centers to handle customer needs. The numbers of trust officers will grow as the population ages and banks compete to manage estates.

Bigger and Bigger Banks

Over the last twenty years, banks began to merge with other banks on an unprecedented scale. This merger mania has resulted in bigger banks, a trend that shows no signs of stopping. As banks are growing larger, banking is rapidly becoming both national and international.

In the past, the McFadden Act of 1927 restricted banks to having branches only in their home state. Strictly interpreted, it barred banks from offering interstate banking services, but they got around this restriction by opening loan-processing offices around the country. They also set up subsidiary companies out of state and offered bank card services to out-of-state customers.

Banks often acquire out-of-state branches when a troubled bank is "married" to an out-of-state bank capable of handling a merger. This means that the government requires the troubled bank to merge with another, more solvent bank. Banks have begun to cross state lines.

As the regulations prohibiting interstate banking have been repealed, competition between banks has heated up as they try to lure customers away from one another. This opens up even more career opportunities for employees who want to work in other areas of the country.

Banks are also international businesses. The world has been called a global village. Corporations with international offices must be able to move money and investments from country to country, twenty-four hours a day. International banking helps them do that.

International banking is possible largely because technology has shrunk the world and its time zones into manageable sizes. A Japanese businessman can purchase a California company without leaving his Tokyo office. The entire transaction can be done by phone and computer.

A major function of international banking is making loans to other governments and foreign companies. Starting in the 1970s, commercial banks opened branches overseas to make loans to foreign borrowers.

Many of the big players in international banking, such as Citibank, create international syndicates of banks to handle huge transactions for clients. Nowadays, when a company needs financing, an international bank can put together a global package.

Although many U.S. banks have retail banking offices overseas, citizens of the country where the branch is located usually staff the offices. The place for Americans in international banking belongs in the high-finance jobs, and an MBA degree is the key to getting one of these overseas positions. Some banks also want employees with expertise in foreign languages, especially Japanese.

Career Pathways

Career opportunities in banking have never been more diverse. Bank employees no longer work in just operations or lending. Bank employees are attorneys, computer programmers, marketers, salespeople, economists, research analysts, and fund managers, among dozens of other jobs. The official workweek ranges from thirty-five to forty hours, but most officers work many more hours than that.

Here are some broad areas of banking you might consider specializing in:

Commercial banking. Commercial bankers serve individuals, small businesses, and governments. They include huge "money center banks" involved in international lending and foreign currency exchange. Regional bank branches appeal to individuals and businesses. They make loans, process employee payrolls, and provide billing services, foreign currency exchange, and funds transfers.

Trust banking. The trust department holds and manages the assets owned by individuals or institutions and manages the money or other assets for the benefit of the customer. For instance, a person can write a will leaving all of his or her assets in trust for heirs. A corporation can set up a trust account for the investment of its employees' pension funds.

Operations and Information Technology. These departments support all the others. They provide record keeping, bookkeeping, and data processing services for the entire organization. Often employees work with computers and other equipment.

Bank administration and accounting. The administrative employees provide supplies, equipment, personnel, and other support functions for all other units. The accounting department creates and maintains financial records and analyzes the financial health of the company.

Public relations and marketing. These employees match customers and their needs with the company's products and services so that the company can make a profit. They research, plan, and implement new products and services and ensure proper delivery to customers. Advertising and community relations usually fall under these areas.

Community banking. Community banks are the small local banks you find throughout the country. If you dislike the competitive environment and bustle of a big-city bank, a community bank may be the perfect place for your banking career.

Credit Unions. Recent legislation has expanded the services credit unions can offer. Many services once reserved for banks are now available through credit unions.

Interview: Rosanne Roberts
Vice President, Morgan Stanley Dean Witter
President, R. M. Roberts and Associates, a San Francisco-based human resources consulting firm specializing in the credit union industry
Interviewer: Donald Summers, banker

Q: What are the hot jobs in banking right now?
A: With all the mergers, the banking industry has become much smaller, and much less stable. The credit union environment, however, is still growing.

There has been a movement within the last few years toward creating investment programs in-house. I have been involved with organizations just starting credit union service organizations and the company that must be established when a credit union wants to create a profitable enterprise. A credit union by definition is nonprofit.

I assist in the hiring of the president, the investment consultants, and the sales assistants who work for the investment consultants.

Q: What entry-level jobs position you for growth in the credit union industry?

A: A sales assistant position could lead to a lucrative career.

Q: What educational background do you look for when hiring for entry-level jobs?

A: Normally, a four-year college degree is preferred. Both a four-year degree and a Certified Financial Planner (CFP) designation are preferred for investment consultant positions. An MBA is preferred for the position of program manager. All of these positions require the National Association of Securities Dealers (NASD) Series 7 and 63 licenses.

Q: What do employers look for when they interview candidates for positions at credit unions?

A: In the position of sales assistant, employers look for service and customer service skills. They also look for attention to detail.

Q: How important are people skills as opposed to technical know-how?

A: People skills are very important because credit unions are extremely service-oriented. You must also understand investments.

Q: What advice would you give a young person just starting out?

A: Get your foot in the door. Get every securities license for a company that will sponsor you. Be willing to take a slightly lower salary with additional compensation based on performance.

Finance: The World of Wall Street

"Competition in the business world is more up for grabs than ever. Incumbents are more threatened as promising new entrants have incredible capital resources available to them, and consumers are more open to switching providers. As a result, there's a need to move quickly, to innovate, to be the first."

—David A. Pottruck, president and co-chief executive officer, Charles Schwab & Co., Inc.

Wall Street jobs involve buying and selling all kinds of things such as stocks, bonds, commodities, options, and even entire companies. The object of the buying and selling is to make money.

Wall Street. The words alone bring to mind images of money. Lots of money.

And power. The kind of power that goes with lots of money.

And glamour. The kind of glamour that goes with power and lots of money.

For some people, Wall Street is the American dream. Wall Street has, in fact, been called the Street of Dreams. But as sometimes happens, the dream can become a nightmare.

If you saw the movie *Wall Street* or read the newspapers about the many insider-trading scandals, you have seen the nightmare side of Wall Street.

It is called greed. And it happens when money and power become more important than principles such as honesty, truth, and fair play. People betray the ethics of the business by using privileged information for personal gain.

By far the majority of people working on Wall Street or in the financial services industry across the nation are honest, extremely hardworking people. Jobs in finance and investments are some of the most difficult jobs to get and keep. Only the best and the brightest have a shot at the top.

Many people in this business say that they have been interested in investments all their lives. That kind of interest is essential. Many Wall Street jobs place tremendous stress on the people doing them. They are fast paced, exhilarating, and, sometimes, exhausting. Some jobs, especially the prestigious jobs in investment banking, require people to work 100 hours a week—more than most jobs in any other industry.

People burn out quickly in some of these jobs, but the potential rewards are as great as the positions are difficult. Annual salaries for some jobs easily reach six figures. Other jobs bring much lower salaries, whereas some give people the opportunity to earn a million dollars a year or more.

But money isn't everything to everyone. There is also the prestige and professional reputation that can be gained by putting together billion-dollar deals.

Wall Street is, literally, a narrow street in lower Manhattan, New York City. It was originally a dirt path with a wall of brush and mud in the Dutch trading post called New Amsterdam. The wall became a wooden fence to keep cows from wandering off, but the cows soon gave way to investors.

Wall Street connected the docks on the Hudson River with the docks on the East River. Trade and commerce traveled along Wall Street, as did early merchants who bought and sold furs, money, and tobacco, among other things. Wall Street became a center for much of that trading.

Wall Street coffeehouses and newspapers became the avenues through which investors could buy securities. The first Congress of the United States met in Federal Hall on Wall Street and authorized the issue of $80 million in government bonds.

By 1792, merchants were keeping small inventories of securities to sell over their counters. In that same year, twenty-four businessmen signed an agreement to trade securities only among themselves. These men are considered the original members of the New York Stock Exchange (NYSE).

At one time, only men worked in Wall Street jobs. The brokerage houses and banks were created by powerful men who gave their business to other powerful men. Many firms were family-owned and passed on from generation to generation. Each firm had its very own clientele and territory.

Today, Wall Street companies aren't just on Wall Street. Charles Schwab & Co., Inc. calls San Francisco its home, and many online firms such as E*Trade and Ameritrade are best reached by their Web site addresses.

Deregulation of banking and fixed commissions has blurred the lines and division of responsibilities between banks and other financial institutions. Competition for customers is keen. New financial products are created to lure customers from one company to another.

Many positions cross the boundaries between banking and brokerage. For instance, an analyst covering health care could work for an investment bank, a commercial bank, a brokerage, or an insurance company.

Do you have to go to New York for a "Wall Street" job? Not necessarily.

Wall Street, USA

Wall Street symbolizes the financial world of the United States. While the heart of that world is the street called Wall Street in Manhattan, every major city in the country has its "Wall Street," which provides opportunities for sharp, hardworking young people to succeed.

Wall Street, New York, is the capital of the financial services industry, and the biggest, most prestigious jobs are there. You can be anywhere and be a Wall Street player, but New York remains the financial capital of the world.

Chicago is the center for commodities, and Boston is the home of many mutual funds. The Web is home to approximately 150 online brokers as of the writing of this book. That number is expected to grow. By 2005, experts predict that 20 million households in the United States will be trading online.

Technology and Wall Street

The explosion of technology has allowed Wall Street to do business in every corner of the world. Face-to-face international conferences are held over the Internet. Multimillion-dollar deals are handled by phone, fax, and modem. Computers have shrunk the country and the world to a manageable size. But one unforeseen result of the information surge has been increased competition from an unexpected segment of the population: Wall Street's own clients.

Clients are able to conduct their own research quickly and efficiently on the Internet. Anyone with a modem can get daily stock quotes or request company profiles, stock reports, financial statements, earnings performance, future earning estimates, and quotes and charts listing or outlining historical stock performance for thousands of companies. Independent online forums aimed specifically at small investors are filled with stock tips and information about companies and their business prospects.

With all of this information easily available, why would anybody pay hefty charges for a full-service financial adviser? Investors who have extensive holdings, who don't have the time to manage their holdings, or who want expert analyses of potential investments still find full-service financial planners valuable and necessary. Discount online brokerages charge a minimal fee to buy and sell stocks over the Internet, allowing customers to bypass traditional full-service brokers and their larger fees. By concentrating on making trades instead of gathering advice, the companies keep their costs low. The number of electronic brokerages is expected to multiply rapidly in the next few years. The stock market is being shaped by the technology, which has radically reduced the time it takes for a stock transaction. Today, more than 20 percent of stock trades are conducted online.

In a 1999 speech, Frank G. Zarb, chairman and chief executive officer of the NASD, said, "The twenty-first century stock market will be multidealer, computerized, technology-driven, and open to all. People will have access to information that they will want to immediately act on. This will occur because technology has eliminated geographic boundaries and created new investing opportunities that appeal to small investors around the world."

Employment Trends

According to the DOL, brokerage firms employ about 80 percent of people in the financial services industry. Today, brokerage firms also offer investment banking services, such as buying and selling initial stock or bond offerings.

Employment in this area is affected by the activity of stock and futures markets, which are directly impacted by the strength of the economy. The industry prospers when the economy is good and is adversely affected by economic downturns. In 1998, the securities industry employed almost 650,000 workers. An additional 100,000 were self-employed.

Sales representatives make up the majority of employees and are called by a variety of titles: brokers, account executives, traders, registered reps, and financial consultants. Securities brokers buy and sell stocks, bonds, and mutual funds; commodity brokers buy and sell futures contracts on things such as agricultural products, energy sources, and metals. Traders actually make sales, matching buyers and sellers. Financial planners give investment advice and manage investment portfolios for clients.

The DOL expects employment in the industry to increase 40 percent by 2008. Investment in the world market and a strong economy in the United States will help fuel this growth. While the growth of online trading will reduce the need for direct contact with traders, brokers, and sales reps, financial planners will be needed to serve those people who want more personalized service.

Automation will double employment of computer scientists, computer engineers, and systems analysts, and will reduce the need for bookkeepers and auditing clerks.

Interview: Sue Oh, CFP
vice president, Morgan Stanley Dean Witter
stockbroker/financial advisor

Q: How did you get into the financial field?
A: I came to America twenty years ago from Korea. I studied English and economics and joined Dean Witter as a file clerk, then worked my way up from new accounts clerk to sales assistant. After taking classes in economics, finance, business and marketing, I became a stockbroker and then a financial advisor.
Q: What skills are important to develop as a retirement planning specialist?
A: You need good people skills. I love to work with people and to help them make money. You have to have

a strong sales ability. A good salesperson is persuasive and can sell him- or herself to potential clients. Besides selling yourself, you have to sell financial services and products. I suggest that a person who is interested in becoming a financial advisor first get a job selling something—computers, rugs, televisions—it really doesn't matter. See if you like it and if you are good at it.

Another important aspect of the job is to educate clients. I'm really a teacher. After I recommend investments, I have to be able to explain why I suggested them. You also have to be a good listener and ask a lot of questions. Last, but not least, you have to have guts to be able to take rejection day after day, and to have patience when things don't go the way you want them to. My average workday is fourteen to seventeen hours.

Q: What services do you provide as a stockbroker and as a retirement planning specialist?

A: I advise my clients on their financial choices and objectives. I trade stocks, bonds, and commodities such as silver bars and gold coins. I provide them with general banking services such as a checking account, and help them with mortgage loans and refinancing.

Q: How do you keep abreast of trends in the industry?

A: Anyone who wants to be successful in this field must be involved in the process of continuing his or her education. I read financial and trade magazines to study political marketing and economic trends. I also spend lots of time on the computer, tracking trends and doing research.

Q: How has the industry changed over the past ten years, and where do you see it going?

A: Years ago, the position of stockbroker was a prestigious one. There weren't too many brokers and they often came from wealthier families. Gradually, it became easier to get into the field if you didn't have family connections. Now, with trading over the Internet, even an eighty-five-year-old grandmother can buy stock.

I see that people who left their stockbrokers to do their own investing a few years ago are starting to come back. Vanity pushed them out because they thought they could do it themselves. But, in a bear market—when the market experiences a downtrend over a long period of time—people need moral support and look for an advisor to talk to about their investment decisions.

Choosing the Right Job in Banking and Finance

3

This chapter will describe the various job opportunities in the fields of banking and finance. Compare your skills and qualifications to those required for each job. When you find a position that interests you, consider what education and training you will need to follow that career path. Also, keep in mind that job titles may vary from company to company.

Accountant and Auditor

Accountants analyze, research, prepare, write, and verify the accuracy of financial statements and reports. They may specialize in certain areas such as taxes, accounting systems, and cash flow management.

Management accountants handle the financial records of the companies they work for, such as banks and brokerages. They provide and analyze the financial information their executives need to make sound decisions. They also prepare the financial reports required by the government, stock exchanges, and the Securities and Exchange Commission (SEC). They work in areas such as taxation, budgeting, cash management, treasury, and investments.

Auditors maintain and examine the financial records of a business to verify accuracy. Internal auditors work for a company and ensure that its financial records are accurate. They also look for areas of waste or where fraud may exist.

Internal auditors objectively weigh a company's internal accounting and compliance procedures to ensure that financial and information systems are accurate and capable of protecting the company from fraud and waste. They review the company's policies and practices to ensure that they meet current laws and government regulations.

Computer software makes these jobs much easier than they previously were. Numbers can be analyzed and printed out in standard formats for reports or rearranged to provide new information. Software reduces the once-tedious work that accountants and auditors had to perform to get the job done.

These jobs require at least a bachelor's degree in accounting or a similar field, and many employers want people with MBAs or CPAs. Familiarity with computers and account software is important.

Beginners often start as assistants, ledger accountants, and junior auditors. Even though they are classified as beginners, these employees need practical experience in the area before being hired.

According to the U.S. Department of Labor, employment of auditors and accountants is expected to grow. The complexity of doing business will increase the demand for people who can develop information on costs, expenditures, taxes, and many other types of financial information. This information is especially critical in the areas of business expansion or foreign investments.

CPAs have more opportunities than accountants and auditors without this prestigious designation. In most states, certified public accountants are accountants who are licensed and regulated. The designation is granted when the candidate passes a difficult, two-part examination and completes thirty hours of coursework beyond a four-year degree. Most applicants must also have some work experience in the field.

Various professional associations of accountants and auditors grant certifications for members who voluntarily meet each association's requirements.

The Institute of Internal Auditors, Inc., confers the designation Certified Internal Auditor (CIA) on graduates of colleges and universities who have two years of experience in the area and pass a four-part exam.

The Information Systems Audit and Control Association offers a Certified Information Systems Auditor (CISA) designation when candidates pass an examination and have five years of experience. The Accreditation Council for Accountancy and Taxation confers three designations—Accredited in Accountancy (AA), Accredited Tax Advisor (ATA), and Accredited Tax Preparer (ATP). Each designation requires candidates to pass an examination and some require coursework. Other organizations, such as the Bank Administration Institute, confer specialized designations.

Accountants and auditors need a good aptitude for math, and the ability to analyze and interpret facts and figures. They also need clear communication skills in both speaking and writing. Accountants and auditors must work with numbers, reports, and financial statements for long periods of time, so concentration abilities are crucial. Employees also need a degree of integrity, since important decisions are made based on the accuracy of the reports they complete.

According to a recent salary survey taken by the National Association of Colleges and Employers, beginning accountants and auditors with bachelor's degrees average $38,000 a year, and people with master's degrees earn an average of $49,500 a year. Experienced people can earn more than $100,000 a year. CPAs may earn even more.

Young people interested in accounting can talk to their colleges' placement centers about the availability of internships and summer jobs in the field.

Bank Teller

The teller is the bank employee with whom most customers regularly come into contact. The teller cashes checks; takes deposits; processes withdrawals; sells savings bonds; accepts payments on utility bills, bank charge cards, and loans; processes the paperwork for certificates of deposit; buys and sells foreign currency; and sells traveler's checks.

But that's not all.

Tellers also take deposits from businesses and balance the money deposited against the amount shown on deposit slips. They make up the bags of money that businesses buy to make change for their customers.

As you might guess, a bank teller must be good with numbers. He or she has to count large amounts of cash accurately. A teller must also be able to use computers and other kinds of office equipment such as adding machines.

Bank tellers must also be able to keep their cool. If the customer also wants to make a deposit, pay a bill, and buy traveler's checks, the teller must apply the same level of accuracy to each transaction. If the customer is in a bad mood, irritated at having to wait in line, or angry over something that has nothing to do with the bank, the teller must also become a master of customer service.

When a customer has multiple transactions, the teller must maintain his or her accuracy while handling a variety of tasks, each requiring a separate set of verifications. For instance, if a customer wants to cash a check, the teller must make sure the written and numerical amounts on the check agree, verify that the person cashing the check is the person to whom it is written, be certain the account on which the check is drawn has enough funds, and count out the money to the customer.

The teller's day starts before the doors of the bank open and it ends long after the last customer is helped. Tellers begin the workday by receiving and counting the cash they will work with that day. They are responsible for making sure the cash balances against all the transactions they handle during the day, and balancing their cash is the last thing they do at the end of their shifts.

Some tellers service the automatic teller machines that receive deposits, issue withdrawals, and take payments by computer.

In addition to all this, tellers are expected to sell new services to their customers, so they must be aware of new products and how customers can use them.

The job lends itself to part-time hours, and college students often work as tellers in local banks because of that flexibility. Many bank officers started their career as a part-time teller while in school.

To become a teller, you need good numerical and clerical skills. You must feel comfortable handling large amounts of money and dealing directly with the public.

Most tellers have a high school diploma, and many are college students.

Tellers are trained both in classes and on the job. They are often paired with experienced tellers who show them the duties of the job.

Tellers can move on to senior teller positions, and many become customer service representatives. Tellers with some college credits can become managers and supervisors.

Teller jobs are among the lower-paying jobs in banking. According to the U.S. Department of Labor, annual earnings for a full-time teller range from $13,000 to $23,000.

Bookkeeper and Accounting Clerk

Bookkeepers and accounting clerks keep financial records, either in ledgers or by computer. They also put together financial statements showing the money that a business receives and pays out, including such items as employee salaries, office expenses, and premiums paid to insurance companies. They may also prepare and mail customers' bills and handle inquiries from suppliers.

33

In large companies, several bookkeepers and clerks usually work for more senior staff members. Each clerk may specialize in a certain area such as preparing statements of income from sales, daily operating expenses, or bills paid and due. In a computerized office, the clerk or bookkeeper enters the financial information into a computer and reviews and balances printouts based on the information. He or she may also review activities performed online.

Working hours are standard, and these jobs lend themselves to part-time work, so they are good for college students.

Employees usually have at least a high school diploma and must have studied principles of accounting and basic business bookkeeping. Many employers are beginning to require that bookkeepers and accounting clerks also complete an accounting program at a junior college. Knowledge of computers and typing is valuable.

Bookkeepers and accounting clerks must be good with numbers and able to concentrate on detailed work. Even small mistakes can be serious.

Bookkeeping and accounting skills are transferable to most other industries, since just about every business needs bookkeepers and accounting clerks.

The salary for full-time bookkeepers and accounting clerks is $22,700 to $34,700.

Broker/Sales Rep/ Financial Consultant

The position of broker is often called by different names within different companies. Institutional brokers help organizations such as insurance companies, retirement funds, and nonprofit organizations to invest their money.

Brokers who serve individuals are called financial consultants, retail brokers, stockbrokers, or account executives. But no matter what a specific company may call them, they are all registered representatives. That means they have passed the New York Stock Exchange securities examination and are licensed to sell securities. In this section we are talking about brokers who serve individuals.

Twenty years ago brokers sold stocks and not much else. Today, brokers help people buy and sell a wide variety of securities, such as stocks, bonds, shares of mutual funds, gold, silver, tax shelters, money market accounts, mortgage financing, and even insurance.

Brokers advise their clients on how to invest their money to meet their financial goals. They also execute buys and sells for their clients' portfolios.

Most brokers want clients who have at least $50,000 to invest. Some won't represent a client who has less than $100,000 to invest. And others may require more than a million dollars from each investor!

Brokers must be certified by several agencies. They must pass an examination that qualifies them to work as a registered representative at the New York Stock Exchange. This is a grueling, six-hour test that can take up to four months to study for.

They also must pass the National Association of Securities Dealers (NASD) test. Many also want commodities and insurance licenses. That means more tests, lots of studying, and, maybe, classes. A broker's firm often helps by supplying study materials and giving or paying for courses.

Once a broker is registered, the employer sends him or her through an internal training program to learn how the company works. The best training is given in the large full-service firms such as Merrill Lynch. Typically, newcomers may put in sixty-five to seventy hours a week just studying and reading about the business and the products and services offered by their company.

A broker is then on his or her own. A broker is given office space, a desk, a phone, and not much else. Even though brokers work for employers, they can set up their own business and hours. Their goal is to build up a client list and generate income for the company and themselves.

Brokers begin with a salary that gets smaller and smaller and eventually vanishes as their time with the company increases. Eventually, brokers live on commissions only, so if they don't sell they don't get paid.

Every time a client uses a broker, the client is charged a commission. Brokers receive between 30 and 50 percent of the commissions their customers bring into the company. For instance, most brokers are expected to gross at least $200,000 in commissions a year. If the broker earns a 30 percent commission, the annual salary is $60,000 ($200,000 X 30 percent).

Brokers who bring in the largest gross commissions receive the largest percentages. There is no ceiling on how much a broker can earn. Million-dollar incomes are not uncommon. On the other hand, brokers who consistently bring in below-average gross commissions may find their percentages decreased.

Brokers spend a lot of time looking for leads—people who might be interested in using their services. In the beginning they make lots of "cold calls"—calling total strangers and trying to persuade them to invest. Leads come from lists of high-income people who buy products such as Mercedes Benz or BMW cars or who buy homes in high-income or upscale areas.

Rejection is all too common in this business. Brokers hear a lot of "No's" before someone says "Yes."

Brokers estimate that it takes about three months of customer contact to land a new client. If the broker does a good job, one client will refer the broker to someone else and the broker's book of contacts will grow. On the average, it takes about two years to build a book of contacts.

Brokers spend their days on the phone calling leads and their evenings visiting clients at home. Each broker must keep up with what his or her clients need, and with new investment products that might meet those needs. Since each broker competes with every other broker on the Street (a term for all of Wall Street), personal service gives a broker an edge over his or her peers.

Competition from discount brokerage firms has cut into full-service brokerages. Many investors are also buying and selling securities directly, using their personal computers. This means that brokerages are losing business, and in response, some firms are considering paying brokers flat salaries rather than commissions.

Basically, a broker is a salesperson. One of the best qualifications for the job is sales experience, regardless of what was sold. In fact, if a would-be broker has spent several years working as a salesperson and has a good sales record, but doesn't have a college degree, he or she still has a good chance of getting a broker's job.

"These employees are often generalists," says Wells Fargo's David Skolnik. "They need to understand estate planning, lending, and insurance planning, among other topics. These jobs require people with excellent attention skills and the ability to ask key questions to understand a client's needs and goals. On the sales side, it takes tenacity and patience along with an understanding of the markets and economy." Salary ranges for brokerage positions range from $31,400 to $103,040.

Interview: George Frankenstein, Vice President of Private Client Services at Donaldson, Lufkin & Jenrette, a New York-based firm.

Q: How did you become a broker?
A: My dad loved the market, and he always talked to me about it. Even when I was a kid and didn't know what I was talking about, I used to ask him how the market was going. It has always been a part of my life.

When I was in college, I realized I wanted to be an entrepreneur; to own my own business. My dad suggested that I visit a brokerage firm about a job. I did, and they hired me.

I spent three years working in the back room, doing just about everything. I learned it all. Then, when I was about twenty-six, I finally started selling. I was the new kid on the block—the youngest broker in the firm.

I'm also the exception to the rule: I worked my way into the job from the back room. Most of the brokers in this business come from other kinds of jobs, usually sales.

Over the twenty-plus years I've been in this business, I've worked at four different firms and built up a steady, regular list of clients, which I have taken with me. That's the good thing about what I do: You're really self-employed.

Q: Can you give a little more detail on that?

A: The brokerage gives you what you need to set up an office—a space, a desk, a phone; then you're on your own. I even brought my secretary with me from the last move, and I pay her myself.

My clients are mine to take with me if I leave. That's different from being an institutional broker. Accounts are assigned to institutional brokers, but the accounts are clients of the firm, not the broker. If the broker leaves, the clients stay and are assigned to a new broker.

This can be a fickle business, and a management change can leave a lot of institutional brokers without a job or clients.

On the other hand, if you are a hot retail broker every brokerage wants you because you bring your clients with you and can produce commissions immediately.

Q: What do you dislike about the job?

A: This is an information business, and some of that information isn't correct. Sometimes, things go sour despite your best intentions. It is very humiliating to tell someone a stock is great based on information you have received, only to have the price drop.

Q: How do you handle the situation when a client loses money?

A: Everybody realizes that there are risks in this business. Sometimes the information you use is bad, or you use bad judgment, or the market in general just drops.

Sometimes you hit it right, and that's the goal: to be right more often than wrong. When you are right, there is no better feeling. I believe that if you are prudent and buy good stocks over a period of time, you will do well.

Q: Do you put together different investments for each of your clients?

A: Yes. The clients' goals are critical. You have to know what they want and what kind of risks they can take. You also want to be sure you and the client match. You can't be all things to all people.

I'm not a big trader. I try to manage people's money for quality growth and income. For instance, I have a client who is a widow. When I started working with her, we put together a portfolio of stocks for her. Last year I made only one trade for her account. Another broker might have made a dozen.

Q: How can a young person best prepare for a job as a retail broker?

A: This is one of the few businesses that you can get into without capital and do well by doing a good job. But there is one thing you do need: sales experience. Spend four to six years out in the real world after college and sell something. It doesn't matter what, just build up a good sales record.

It's not critical to get a business education. In my opinion, all you really need is accounting courses so you can read financial statements. You can learn everything else you need to know by reading.

Pick three or four financial publications and read them consistently to build up a bank of knowledge. Learn to talk intelligently about the industry.

You need to create a context for the information you receive. You also need a point of reference for making judgments.

I had recommended that a client buy shares of Bank of America stock when it was around $13 a share. The client was so annoyed with the recommendation that he pulled his account. Bank of America stock went down to $7, then the company turned around and the stock is now above $25. I knew Bank of America was going to succeed.

You pick up that kind of knowledge by learning as much as you can about industries and companies. You learn how to make solid judgments. My clients depend on my judgment, and that's a lot of responsibility. You carry the business with you all the time. I never really get a vacation. I call in every day when I'm not here.

Q: Any last advice?

A: If you want to be a broker, become well-informed, provide a prudent service over and above the average broker, and keep your customers' needs in mind.

Clerical Supervisor and Manager

Clerical support employees keep their companies running smoothly by keeping the paperwork moving. Clerical supervisors and managers interview potential employees and either recommend who should be hired or actually do the hiring. They welcome new employees and orient them to the company, and they may also train employees or oversee their training by another employee.

Supervisors and managers must be familiar with the duties of all the jobs that report to them. They make assignments so that the work gets done every day, and they juggle those assignments among employees when someone is absent. So they must understand the strengths and weaknesses of their employees. They also evaluate employee performance and help poor performers improve. They usually can recommend promotions, awards, salary increases, firings, and transfers.

Supervisors and managers monitor workflow to make sure that deadlines are met and that any problems are identified and resolved right away. Most supervisors and managers hold meetings with their employees to make sure everyone works toward the same goals.

When problems arise, supervisors and managers take on the responsibility of solving them. That may mean counseling employees with problem behaviors, retraining employees, or changing procedures.

Clerical supervisors and managers report to their managers about how the work is moving and whether their deadlines are being met. No matter what happens, the work must get done. That's their job.

In addition to personnel and workflow matters, clerical supervisors and managers also decide what office equipment their employees need, such as computer terminals, typewriters, and workstations.

If a company is covered by a union contract, the supervisor and manager must understand what is in the contract and abide by its terms in the running of their departments.

Most clerical supervisors and managers work forty-hour weeks, but many take work home to keep current. Often, a business requires round-the-clock operation, so some supervisors and managers work swing or grave-yard shifts and many draw extra pay for night work.

These jobs are not entry-level positions. Most clerical supervisors and managers are promoted from within the company or are recruited from other companies. They must demonstrate a solid knowledge of job duties and the ability to supervise people, follow orders, deal with stress, and balance the needs of their managers and their employees.

Good supervisors and managers are efficient and use time to their advantage. They organize work and set priorities well. Many have bachelor's degrees, and most larger companies either offer in-house developmental classes or reimburse supervisors and managers for the fees they pay for outside education. Salaries range from $21,800 to $48,600.

Commercial Banker

While commercial banks have moved into new areas such as discount brokerage, insurance, and investments, most banks still concentrate on lending or wholesale banking. Government organizations, domestic and foreign countries, and private corporations are typical customers who use a wide variety of banking services, often borrowing money to finance their growth. They need bank accounts that allow them to deposit money and earn interest on it while it is not in use. They also use a bank to process and issue paychecks for their employees.

Commercial bank loan officers are key players in maintaining good customer relationships. They determine a customer's credit worthiness—the customer's ability to pay back borrowed money. They do this by studying a company's financial statements, its position in the industry, and many other factors.

Loan officers work closely with customers to determine their financial needs so they can sell them bank products and services that meet those needs.

Loan officers in most banks specialize in a certain kind of customer, such as small businesses, foreign governments, cities, and domestic corporations. Some bankers specialize in industries, for instance, the auto industry or real estate. Entire groups within the bank may be organized to serve these customers.

In the international area, bankers also handle the financial needs of foreign companies and domestic companies that have overseas units. Part of their job is to protect their clients from the adverse effects of foreign currency exchanges.

Many banks have what is called a new business group. The employees in this area actively look for new businesses in which they can sell the bank's products and services. They rely less on cold calls (calling strangers to ask for business) than on obtaining recommendations from existing customers or their current contacts.

Competition is keen among banks, and it is necessary for each bank to set itself apart from the others. That means providing personal service. Commercial bankers may entertain their clients with lunches, dinners, and tickets to events.

Most financial services companies offer training programs for commercial banking. The program may last a few months to a few years, and it may rotate trainees in all positions, or put each trainee in a specific area for the entire training period.

Some banks design training programs to eliminate the bottom 10 percent of the class; other banks want to keep all their trainees. It is important to find out the nature of the program and its attrition rate.

Salaries start in the low twenties for trainees and move up at a steady, if not spectacular, rate. You will need a bachelor's degree and an MBA if you are interested in foreign banking.

Interview: Catherine Lam, vice president, Appraisal Department, Sanwa Bank

Q: What is your background?

A: I have a bachelor's in economics. Appraising is not a highly specialized profession at the onset. I know appraisers who have college degrees in history, art, math, and other fields. Appraising calls on a number of skills that are common to everybody, but also requires some training. Most people learn appraising on the job from another appraiser.

Q: What do you do?

A: I am a staff appraiser. I appraise property that is potential collateral for a loan. Sanwa Bank is a construction lender, so I often appraise something that isn't built yet. I look at the plans and try to visualize what it would be worth if it were already built. The bank needs that information to decide whether it will lend money on the project. I'm the loan officer's eyes and ears.

Q: What do you have to know to perform appraisals?

A: You wear a lot of hats. You have to think like a tenant, developer, investor, leasing agent, and architect.

You have to be able to read leases and contracts, survey the market, research the demand for the type of structure being constructed, read plans, determine what the building will rent for. That's just part of what you have to research before you can submit your conclusions to the loan department.

You are an investigator building a case and supporting what you believe is the value. The bottom line is that you are expressing an opinion. Sometimes you have to argue it with the loan officer or the leasing agent.

Q: Does the job end after the appraisal is completed?

A: No. I may have to reappraise the property if the loan term needs an extension, or if there is a problem with the loan. For construction loans, I may also need to periodically inspect the property to report on the construction progress and recommend loan fund disbursements.

Q: How did you start in the business?

A: I started appraising houses and then moved into commercial and industrial properties.

Q: How far can you go?

A: Some appraisers can open their own business or become a chief appraiser and run the department. Some become consultants, performing feasibility studies.

Q: What do you like about the job?

A: Job satisfaction comes from knowing your market and being able to substantiate what you believe. I like analyzing the data and finding hard evidence to support my opinion. You're constantly in the market, talking to brokers, buyers, and sellers. Every property is different. The hours are flexible. You spend time out of the office every week, although residential property appraisers spend more time outside than commercial appraisers do.

Q: How has technology changed the job?

A: Computers and the Internet have made research, writing, and calculating value much more efficient. But it does not substitute for the ability to look dispassionately at the data and make a reasonable value estimate.

Commodity Trader

Commodities are the things that make the world go round. Sugar, salt, wheat, gold, corn, coffee, hogs, cattle, silver, lumber, oil—the list is almost endless. And savvy investors buy and sell each and every one of these items, hoping to make a profit.

Commodities trading began in 1848 when eighty-two businessmen formed the Chicago Board of Trade. The heart of commodities trading is still in Chicago, but anyone, anywhere, can trade in commodities.

Commodities, more than any other investment, depend on circumstances such as weather, natural disasters, and world events. A drought in the Midwest may mean that farmers grow less wheat. The price of wheat soars. A military coup in a coffee-growing country sends coffee prices soaring. An oil spill in Alaskan waters pushes up the prices of oil and gasoline.

Commodities involve futures and options.

If a producer sees a book he thinks will make a good movie, he options it. That means he buys the rights to make a movie from the book by a certain date in the future. While the option is in effect, no one else can make a movie from that book. If the movie isn't made, the option can be renewed or dropped. If it is dropped, another producer can option it.

The commodities market operates similarly. You buy an option to buy a commodity at a certain future date. It is like placing a bet that the price for your commodity will go up or down. If you think it will go up, you buy a call option. If you think it will go down, you sell a put option.

With a futures contract, you decide to buy or sell a specific amount of a certain commodity by a set date in the future.

This is how commodity investing works:

Let's say you buy wheat from a farmer, then sell it to a baker. Your profit comes from the spread, the difference between what you paid for the wheat and what you sell it for. On one hand, if you buy the wheat at $2 a pound, but the wheat crop that year is very good, you might have to sell it for $1.50 a pound because everyone else is selling wheat, too, and, as a result, the price has been driven down. In this case, you lose money—50 cents on the pound. On the other hand, if the wheat crop is thin that year, wheat is at a premium and you might be able to sell it for $3 a pound. Now, you make a profit.

You can also buy the right to buy wheat the farmer hasn't grown yet. You promise to pay a certain amount of money for the wheat at harvest time, hoping you can sell it for a higher price when the time comes. That is a description of futures trading.

Or, you can buy an option. You pay the farmer 25 cents a pound for the right to buy his wheat for a specific amount per pound within a certain amount of time. He keeps your option money whether you buy the wheat or not.

As you can see, commodities are pretty tricky investments. But investors can make a million dollars on one smart move.

Commodity traders have seats on commodities exchanges. The number of seats is limited, and the price of a seat is usually several hundred thousand dollars. Buying a seat gives the trader the right to buy and sell commodities without using a broker and paying commissions. Traders can lease a seat for $60,000 to $70,000.

The trading floor is called The Pit, and it is a no-holds-barred place. Polite behavior and manners have no place in The Pit. It is a rough-and-tumble environment.

Newcomers start out in The Pit as runners and clerks, earning up to $46,000 a year. After they learn the ropes, they can buy or lease a seat. They also need about $25,000 in cash to trade for their own account.

Traders use a clearing agent, a person who charges them per contract and who functions as a bank. The agent provides capital, an office, and secretarial support, and may even give traders employee benefits.

Traders specialize in certain commodities, often buying and selling contracts within minutes of each other. They can make a fortune one minute, and lose it the next.

Traders often make six-figure incomes—not bad for a job that doesn't require a college degree.

Computer Specialist

Years ago, a company's computer occupied an entire room. Today, entire rooms are still devoted to data processing, but the computers are smaller, lighter, and faster than ever before.

Computers allow financial businesses and banks to store and manipulate millions of pieces of information and documents online. Perhaps more than any other recent innovation, computers have made international banking and finance a reality.

People thousands of miles apart can conduct extremely sophisticated transactions without leaving their offices. Computers can be used to itemize accounts, create research reports, quote the prices of securities worldwide, and project results of investments based on several variables.

On the Nasdaq stock market alone, between one billion and two billion shares are traded each day. Computers handle it all.

This means that career opportunities have never been better for computer operators and operators of peripheral equipment such as printers and disk drives.

The rise of information technology means that all businesses need a variety of computer specialists—skilled employees who can design and maintain hardware and software and develop new, innovative applications for existing programs. These workers are called by a variety of names and perform a variety of functions—computer systems analysts, engineers, scientists, database administrators—in addition to computer operators who manage and maintain peripheral equipment such as printers.

These jobs are expected to grow quickly, and most new jobs will be created in this area. Work experience and a bachelor's degree are required for more complex jobs such as analyst and database administrator. A graduate degree is necessary for many engineering and scientific jobs. However, computer support specialists and operators often learn on the job.

Because some programs run for twenty-four hours, most computer jobs involve shift work, and they are often staffed seven days a week. In addition to businesses in banking and finance, most industries that must maintain large amounts of customer or employee data—such as insurance companies, hospitals, and colleges—use computer operators. The job offers the opportunity to change employers and industries.

Many companies train computer operators on the job, and clerical workers from other areas have the opportunity to transfer into this position. Many high schools, vocational schools, business schools, and community colleges offer courses in computer operations.

Most employers want people with at least a high school diploma. Some prefer employees with data processing experience. Salaries range from the low teens to $80,000 a year.

Customer Service Representative

With the rise of new technologies, companies are turning to call centers to handle customer inquiries and problems. In fact, as more and more transactions are performed electronically, personalized customer service becomes more important. There are times when a customer needs to talk to someone who can answer a question or resolve a problem. In response, companies are hiring more customer service representatives.

Call centers are often full-fledged customer service centers staffed by hundreds of employees who spend their time answering telephone calls and responding to e-mails from customers. They research the customers' problems and handle complaints. Call centers themselves are technology-driven. Customer service representatives can access customers' accounts on demand and perform real-time services.

Many customer service jobs don't require formal training, although reps need in-depth knowledge of systems, procedures, and policies in order to answer questions and resolve problems.

People skills are most important, as is the ability to handle difficult, often angry callers. Customer service reps can experience stressful situations that require

51

them to remain calm and courteous. In addition to people skills, more businesses are requiring a higher level of technical expertise, particularly for customer service reps who are responding to problems associated with online transactions. Starting salaries average $22,000 a year. Call center managers earn more than $100,000 a year.

Economist

Economists study how a society uses resources such as labor, raw materials, and machinery to produce goods and services, and they look at the benefits and costs of distributing and using these goods and services.

Economists use mathematical theories to explain the reasons for business cycles or inflation, to predict the effects of events such as taxation or unemployment, or to study and analyze consumer spending trends. They then use their theories to advise businesses in many industries, including banking and finance.

Economists, to a certain extent, try to predict the future based on existing information and trends. Some types of predictions they may be asked to make involve what new products and services should be developed and how they should be priced and marketed; how a company should diversify its operations; whether a new branch should be opened; and the forecast of foreign or domestic economic conditions.

Economists obtain the information they need to make their recommendations and forecasts in several ways. They may conduct surveys; develop models for projections; review and analyze reports, articles, tables, statistics, charts, and any other pertinent documents;

and interview experts in those areas. They then put together reports of their results in clear, readable terms.

Often, economists work under great pressure and tight deadlines, juggling several research reports at one time.

Most economists work for private companies such as banks, investment firms, brokerages, and insurance companies. Most work in large cities, usually in the home offices of their companies since their work directly affects decisions made at the highest levels of the organization.

Beginning economists need a bachelor's degree in either economics or marketing, with courses in microeconomics, macroeconomics, business cycles, economic and business history, economic development, money and banking, and marketing, among others. A strong background in mathematics, statistics, survey design, and computer science is helpful. Advancement to senior economist positions requires a graduate degree in economics. Starting salaries average around $26,500 per year for economists with a bachelor's degree and around $31,600 per year for those with a degree in economics. Economists with a Ph.D. can earn more than $90,000 a year.

The U.S. Department of Labor projects that the need for economists will grow faster than many other occupations through the end of the century. The best opportunities can be found in the financial services industry, which also pays the highest salaries.

File Clerk

Despite the wide use of computers, files must still be maintained in all businesses. File clerks are responsible for maintaining and updating accurate records. They classify, store, update, and retrieve material and identify and file new material.

Files can be maintained either by subject, alphabetical order, or numerical order. Files are usually maintained in either a paper or microfilmed format.

File clerks may also perform miscellaneous clerical duties such as typing, photocopying, or opening, sorting, and posting mail.

File clerks must be able to type and do accurate paperwork. Good spelling is essential, as is neatness.

Employers prefer candidates with a high school education. Training usually occurs on the job, since each company has its own system.

File clerk jobs are entry-level positions, and most employers look for people who demonstrate an ability to learn, assume additional responsibilities, and, eventually, move on to other jobs. Annual earnings average around $19,000.

Financial Manager

Financial managers are called by a variety of titles such as treasurer, controller, or cash manager, according to their primary responsibility.

Because banks and other financial services companies handle cash and securities, financial managers are needed in many areas. Managers must be totally familiar with the laws and regulations governing the industry and their particular area. They must also have a working knowledge of other areas, and some need a thorough understanding of the financial systems, laws, and regulations of foreign countries.

Basically, financial managers prepare the financial reports that a company issues to comply with laws and government regulations and oversee the flow of cash into and out of a company.

In large firms, financial managers may also consult with other managers, lawyers, economists, and other financial professionals to develop, implement, and monitor financial policies and procedures.

The controller manages the accounting, audit, and budget departments and directs the research and preparation of financial reports such as income statements and balance sheets.

Cash managers control the flow of money. They monitor and recommend investments of the company's money to ensure that financial goals are met.

Risk and insurance managers minimize losses and risks that come from the financial transactions in which the company engages.

Credit managers establish credit criteria and monitor the company's use and extension of credit.

A bachelor's degree in accounting, finance, or business is required, and with many employers an MBA is essential for advancement. Knowledge of computers and a variety of financial services such as banking, insurance, and securities is important.

Most often, financial managers work their way up in the organization, although a company may hire an experienced financial manager from a competitor if no qualified candidate is available internally. Good candidates for financial manager jobs are accountants; budget, credit, or securities analysts; and loan officers.

Experienced financial managers can work in just about any industry, so the opportunity to move around and advance is good. Many financial managers also establish their own consulting firms.

The U.S. Department of Labor estimates that the need for financial managers will grow over the next few years, especially as competition, government reporting regulations, and the complexity of financial services increase. Competition for the best jobs will also be keen. Annual salaries are in the low $100,000's, including bonuses.

Financial Planner

Financial planning is a fairly new career path. It began in the 1960s, but it was not until 1972 that the nation's first financial planning curriculum was established with the College for Financial Planning.

When the banking industry was deregulated, banks introduced a variety of financial products to lure customers away from their competitors. Non-bank industries such as insurance companies, stock-brokers, and even retailers introduced investment products and services.

Today's financial environment is much more complicated than ever before, and investors must understand inflation, changing tax laws, the need for retirement planning, complicated employee benefit plans, and thousands of financial products—or hire professionals who do understand them.

The average person cannot begin to know all the options available. That is where the financial planner comes in. There are too many variables for the average person to consider.

Financial planners help people invest their money. They analyze a client's financial status and fitness and create an investment plan to help the client reach his or her financial goals. A financial plan can include ways to lower taxes, increase investment income, provide adequate insurance coverage, and plan for retirement.

According to Dr. William L. Anthes, former president of the College for Financial Planning, in Denver, Colorado, "To accommodate the needs of various clients and understand the sophisticated array of financial products available in the marketplace, a financial planner must have both technical training and professional experience."

In a survey of financial planners conducted by the college, respondents stated that the most important subjects that planners needed to master were listening and speaking skills, knowledge of ethical standards and practices, financial planning and investment planning processes, and tax laws.

The financial planner may be a generalist, trained in many different areas. He or she must understand insurance, taxes, employee benefit plans, investments, individual retirement accounts, and trust funds, among other financial programs and products. A financial planner can also coordinate the work of other financial professionals such as accountants, tax attorneys, lawyers, and bankers.

Often, a planner has a degree in accounting, economics, business administration, or finance. Planners who deal in securities must have a license or be registered with the Securities and Exchange Commission or the National Association of Securities Dealers (NASD).

The Division of Insurance or a similar state agency should license planners who handle insurance products where that planner does business.

According to the College for Financial Planning, career opportunities are "seemingly endless." You can specialize in any number of areas such as accounting, insurance, securities, banking, or law.

You can practice anywhere in the country. You can work independently or within a company.

No federal standards govern financial planners. Anyone can call himself or herself a planner and advertise for clients. But, there are professional organizations that require a level of education and professional expertise before admitting planners to membership.

Just about everyone needs a financial plan of some kind. The simplest plan is a budget. Generally, the more money one earns, the more financial decisions must be made. Most people work for employers that provide employee benefit plans, which require more decisions. Truly wealthy people have fortunes to protect and multiply.

A client consults a financial planner for many of the following reasons:

- To choose investments for a specific goal such as a child's college education, a home down payment, or a retirement nest egg
- To reduce taxes
- To obtain the right amount and kind of insurance protection
- To integrate employee benefit plans with personal investment and insurance plans
- To maximize investment earnings
- To organize finances
- For estate planning

Many planners specialize. Some handle only wealthy or upscale clients with a financial worth of several hundred thousand dollars. Others work with people just starting their careers. Many are self-employed; some work for corporations or small businesses that specialize in certain areas of finance.

A planner pulls together all of his or her client's financial information and future goals by working with the client to complete a detailed questionnaire. He or she must know exactly where the client is financially and where the client wants to go.

The planner also must assess each client's "risk quotient"—the ability to handle risk. Some clients want only safe investments such as government bonds and insured savings vehicles such as time certificates of deposit.

Other clients are willing to take large risks such as providing capital for start-up businesses or investing in the options market.

Most people probably fall in between and are willing to run the risks associated with investing in stocks and bonds, mutual funds, and other uninsured, but relatively safe, investments.

The planner then studies all this information and puts together an investment plan. The plan includes recommendations for financial investments, insurance, and taxes. But that is not the end of it.

The planner must constantly update the financial plan as the economy and the client's personal situation changes to make sure that the plan remains true to the client's goals and accurately reflects the client's financial status.

Some planners merely complete the plan; others help the client to implement it by actually making the investments and purchasing the products they have recommended.

The annual starting salary for a financial planner is $37,300, but some planners earn more than a million dollars a year. Financial planners earn their income in several ways. Some charge hourly fees or flat fees. Some promote certain products and services and are paid a commission when they sell those products or services to investors. Others combine both commissions and fees.

Flat fees vary according to the complexity of the plan. If you work for a company, the plan usually takes into account investment or insurance products offered by your employer.

The program offered by the College for Financial Planning teaches all areas of personal financial planning. It is a two-year course of study leading to the professional designation. This program was the nation's first formal financial-planner program and has earned widespread recognition and respect.

The College for Financial Planning offers several degrees, including a designation of Certified Financial Planner (CFP). After completing the course, graduates receive the CFP designation from the Institute of Certified Financial Planners. After the degree is granted, members must complete at least thirty additional units of study each year.

Most candidates already have college degrees. To qualify for the program, you must have at least three years of professional experience in personal financial planning or a closely related area of the financial services industry such as insurance, banking, accounting, or investments. If you have less than three years of experience, you can enroll with provisional status until you fulfill the three-year requirement.

Many colleges and universities also offer courses, certificates, and undergraduate and graduate programs in financial planning and investments.

A candidate for a financial-planning program needs a knack for detail, a sense of organization, good problem-solving skills, the ability to work well with people, and good listening and communication skills.

Most of the planners enrolled in the College of Financial Planning hold bachelor's degrees, and some have received graduate degrees. Degrees in accounting, finance, business, or a related area provide a good foundation. However, some students enrolled in the CFP program have only a high school diploma, so it is possible to become a planner without a formal college education. The college also offers a paraplanner program for people who provide support services to planners.

Interview: Judy Miller, CFP
principal, College Solutions

Q: How did you move from being a stockbroker to finding a niche as an education and financial services planner?
A: I was working at Citibank, where I sold mutual funds to preferred clients (those with portfolios between $100,000 and $2 million). When I decided to go out on my own, I realized that my shoulders were not broad enough to expertly handle all the complex services and products in the financial market. I decided to specialize.
Q: Why focus on this niche in financial planning?
A: Many people today postpone having children until they are established in their careers. Soon enough, they find

themselves having to think about putting their teenage children through college at a time when their own retirement is not far off. I've watched many people make poor financial decisions under those circumstances.

I have a master's degree in education and I taught high school English before I went into financial planning. I love working with young people! I decided to combine being a college counselor and a financial planner.

Q: What services do you offer to your clients?

A: I counsel families on college options, taking into account each family's financial situation and the student's career goals. The average college education costs at least $250,000. I want both parents and students to understand the financial options they have, and how decisions they make now will affect their current and future financial situation.

I provide financial planning needs by looking at how investments impact college education; for example, insurance, disability, estate/tax/retirement planning, and cash flow.

I also have built my business by marketing my services to other financial planners who refer their clients to me specifically for college financial-planning purposes.

Q: What do you see in the future of financial planning?

A: I think that life values will become a very important part of financial planning. If having lots of money doesn't help fulfill a person's life, what good is it? As wealth builds, people begin to think about what they want their lives to have stood for. I'm beginning to do what I call values-based intergenerational coaching. For example, grandparents' gifts can positively or negatively affect, dollar for dollar, how much financial aid a child is eligible to receive, depending on how it's invested.

Q: How is financial planning changing?

A: It's becoming more mature and respected in its own right as a profession. Expectations of clients are more complex now and investors need comprehensive financial management services. More consumers are realizing the importance of seeking an advisor who has a Certified Financial Planner's license.

Q: What attributes does one need to become a financial advisor?

A: Ultimately, money is integral to everyone's existence. We spend money on what we want. I help people learn what they want—often, they don't know themselves. To do that, you need to have very strong people skills, and the ability to listen well and formulate questions.

Q: What other advice can you give a person considering a career as a financial advisor?

A: Just because you're not a numbers person, don't let that discourage you from a career in finance. Of course, you need to know some math, but for certain careers, such as financial planning, you don't need to know a lot of math. It's better to be good with people.

Human Resources

Matching the best employees to available jobs is important to a company's success. Human resources professionals establish policies and procedures for employment, compensation, benefits, and training.

In companies where employees are represented by unions, the human resources professionals may be involved in contract negotiations and may represent the company in grievance hearings. In companies without union representation, human resources professionals often act as liaisons between employees and management. The ability to deal with people at all levels of the company is a critical skill.

Recruiter

Recruiters scout college campuses and other companies for potential employees. They often travel around the country to speak to qualified people to fill vacancies. They must be completely familiar with the company so they can evaluate a prospective employee's skills relative to jobs. They must also be able to discuss all personnel policies, training programs, and promotional opportunities within the company.

Equal Employment Opportunity (EEO) Representative

These employees ensure that plans to hire and promote minority employees are implemented. They resolve EEO grievances, look for violations of antidiscrimination policies and submit EEO reports.

Job Analyst

Analysts compile information on job duties so that detailed job descriptions can be prepared. The descriptions include information on the training or skills required to do the job.

Compensation Manager

A compensation manager develops a company's pay policies and ensures that the company is competitive and can hire the best employees. They conduct salary surveys to see where the company's salaries are relative to other companies.

Benefits Manager

Benefits managers design employee benefit programs to attract and retain qualified employees. This can include putting together cost-effective health care, life insurance, disability, and retirement programs for employees at all levels of the company. The benefits area is highly regulated, and benefits managers must understand how various laws and regulations affect their plans and companies.

Training Manager

Training managers design programs to train new employees, to retrain employees whose jobs are eliminated, and to develop management potential. Training can be technical, designed to teach skills needed to perform specific jobs, such as lending or analyzing stocks. It can also be general, such as time management or supervision.

In large companies, many different employees perform these duties, but in small companies one or two people may be responsible for all of them.

A bachelor's degree is necessary for most jobs. Exposure to liberal arts, psychology, business, and economics is important, but the choice of major is not critical. Many companies maintain personnel records on computers, and human resources employees should be familiar with computers and data processing.

Yearly salaries vary widely by type of job and company, ranging from less than $27,000 to more than

$161,468 paid to senior people who direct entire functions within the human resources area.

Institutional Broker

Institutional account executives are brokers to companies and institutions with large amounts of money to be invested and large portfolios to be managed. They act as middle persons between customers and the research analysts who work for the investment company. They are assigned to a variety of customers and handle mutual funds, retirement funds, and trust funds. Their customers belong to the company they work for; if the broker leaves, the customers are reassigned to another broker.

The account executive recommends which stocks and bonds to buy for the institution's portfolio based on the research done by the analysts. Part of the account executive's job is to visit clients regularly and encourage them to buy the securities recommended by the research analysts.

The buys and sells are executed by the brokerage, which earns a commission on the transactions. One of the account executive's goals is to earn commissions for his or her brokerage.

If an analyst's opinions on a stock change, the account executive immediately notifies his or her customers with recommendations either to buy or to sell the stock. Unlike retail brokers who specialize in certain stocks, industries, or other kinds of investments, institutional brokers must be generalists. They need to be familiar with all the stocks the company's research analysts follow. In some companies that can mean thousands of different stocks. A new account executive can spend several months reading research reports.

Electronic technology, such as computers, modems, and fax machines have made it easier for institutional clients to deal directly with a brokerage's research analysts. Some experts think this trend will make the broker's job less important in the future.

An MBA is usually required, and salaries average $300,000 a year. Top brokers can earn over a million dollars annually.

Investment Banker

Investment banking is "the job" in banking and finance. It is the most glamorous, the most competitive, the most difficult job to get.

Investment bankers help businesses grow. As a company grows, it usually reaches a time when it needs more money than it can raise on its own. The company may not want to borrow from a bank because it does not want to incur a debt that must be paid back with interest. Instead, the company wants to raise permanent capital by issuing stocks or bonds. (Bonds are debts, but usually the company has many more years to repay the debt than it has with a bank loan.)

Investment bankers help companies raise capital. Traditionally, investment bankers match companies that need money with companies that want to invest money. Their jobs and clients take them around the world.

The investment banker may decide that a private placement is called for. Capital is raised by making an offer to a private investor or investors.

Investment bankers also help take companies public. They help their client companies raise money by issuing shares of stocks or bonds or packages of both. The bankers decide when to go public and what to charge for the securities.

These securities are sold to individuals who buy only a few hundred shares or to institutions that may buy thousands of shares. The result can bring millions of dollars of capital to the client company.

The investment banker decides what is the best solution to the client's problem. Once a decision is made, the investment bank handles the transactions. They prepare the legal documents required and file them with the government and securities agencies. These documents must be completely accurate. There is no room for error, and an important, time-consuming part of the process involves researching, writing, and managing the printing and filing of these documents.

Investment banking is a team activity. Each team is made up of three to five people, including analysts, associates, and a managing director. Analysts and associates (entry-level employees) may work on more than one team. They gather and compile most of the information needed for the offering, double- and triple-checking the numbers until they are certain they are correct. The team also works closely with the company's legal and accounting staffs.

Usually, a larger team is also formed. Called a syndicate, it is made up of other investment banks invited by the original bank to participate in the venture. Each member bank of the syndicate agrees to underwrite a certain amount of the securities being offered. Underwriting banks guarantee payment for the securities.

The originating investment bank may form yet another team called a selling group. The selling group is made up of other investment banks and brokerages that agree to help sell the securities. The selling group does not guarantee that the securities will be sold.

Once all the government and state approvals are granted, the offering is made to the institutional and retail clients of the underwriting investment banks and the banks and brokerages in the selling group.

Part of the selling effort involves going on the road. Investment bankers and institutional brokers tour major cities and give presentations on the offering to institutional investors.

Because the Glass-Steagall Act bars banks from underwriting securities, they engage in investment banking only to underwrite noncorporate securities. For example, a commercial bank may underwrite a bond issue to finance a city library or a new facility on a college campus. They can also give investment advice and arrange for private placements. Banks compete with brokerages and investment banking firms that can, by law, offer a full range of investment banking services.

Investment bankers make money on the spread, the difference between what they pay for the securities and what they sell them for. They make a profit if the price of the security exceeds what they paid for it in the days following the offering. They can also realize a loss if the price falls below the original buying price. Millions of dollars can be gained or lost in a day.

Today, investment bankers also offer advice on mergers and acquisitions—takeovers of one company by another. They give financial advice to companies that want to sell a subsidiary or division, and to governments and foreign countries.

No one does everything; there is too much to know for one person to be able to handle it all. Some investment bankers specialize in certain types of business such as mergers and acquisitions, private placements, or real estate. Some bankers are generalists and become experts in certain industries such as health care. Public finance specialists work with governments and municipalities.

The business of investment banking is complicated, the environment in which the bankers work is highly competitive, and their primary business is selling their services.

Today, investment bankers are salespeople. They must develop relationships with customers and potential clients, and they must cultivate existing relationships. Millions of dollars are to be made, and each investment bank wants a piece of that wealth.

According to Meryl Gordon, former economics reporter for Gannett News Service, "With potential fees so high, investment bankers aren't content to just sit back and wait for business to come in. They go out and make it happen, searching out undervalued companies and touting them to likely acquirers, setting the wheels of merger in motion. While their gyrations may destroy thousands of jobs and devastate whole communities, these Wall Street dealers are totally sheltered from the consequences of their actions. It's an amoral game: Whoever ends up with the most deals and dollars wins."

Thousands of the best and brightest graduates of the nation's best business schools compete for a handful of jobs each year. What is so wonderful and attractive about a business that requires people to work eighty to one hundred hours a week, all year long? Glamour. Prestige. The chance to make a million-dollar income.

Investment bankers earn millions of dollars on billion-dollar deals. For instance, when Philip Morris bought out General Foods for $5.6 billion, the three investment bankers that put the package together split $24.3 million in commissions. An investment banker's bonus can easily double his or her salary.

That kind of money can be tempting to some, and investment banking has recently reeled under the impact of major insider-trading scandals.

The information that financial people obtain about companies or securities cannot be used for personal gain until that information is made public. Nor can the information be given to someone else to use for gain. When this rule is violated, the federal government is swift to prosecute the offenders.

Financial companies work hard to make sure that insider information does not pass between their investment banking and trading departments to ensure that insider-trading laws are not broken.

You can come to investment banking from three directions: directly from college as an analyst; with an MBA; or transferring in from the legal, management consulting, or accounting fields.

The investment banking entry-level jobs offer one of the steepest learning curves on Wall Street. And while some companies offer formal training, much of the work is learned on the job—you either sink or swim.

Analysts (entry-level positions for recent college graduates) can earn $40,000 a year to start. Bonuses can raise that to a whopping $80,000 by the end of the analyst's second year.

Morgan Stanley designed the position of analyst less than forty years ago. Other firms quickly picked up the idea. The job offers recent college graduates with a bachelor's degree an opportunity to spend two years with an investment bank before returning to school for their MBAs. This is one job in which you cannot go to school at night. You will be working most nights.

Almost any undergraduate field of study will do for the analyst program. In fact, many recruiters prefer liberal-arts majors. But do not underestimate the value of computer, accounting, and business courses. They give you the edge in this highly competitive arena.

Research analysts are the gofers of investment banking. Usually, each analyst is part of three- or four-person teams, with each team working on a different project.

The analyst spends lots of time crunching numbers. Part of the job is to analyze a company and its position in its industry. That means studying endless financial reports and accounting records.

Analysts also perform secretarial duties. They proofread documents and spend hours at photocopying machines putting together reports.

Some companies move their analysts around, exposing them to various specialties. In other companies, analysts stay in the area where they start.

Despite the money and prestige, many analysts drop out of the program. As one dropout says, "I was prepared to work like crazy. What I wasn't prepared for was working around the clock and being bored to tears by what I was doing."

To continue in investment banking, most people need an MBA. A few rare superstars are offered associate positions directly out of their analyst training.

Most MBA programs prefer candidates who have had practical business experience, and the analyst programs offered by investment banks fill that requirement nicely.

New MBAs arrive as junior members and join the ranks of the gofers for their first year or two. Then they move up and begin to take on more responsibility.

MBAs start between $80,000 and $100,000 and usually make more than $100,000 by the end of their second year. You can get a vice presidency and make $300,000 (or a million if you are very good) by age thirty.

The grueling, demanding hours and hard work do not lighten up, however, as you move up in the firm. That is one reason investment banking has been called a young person's business. It takes youth to handle the stress and labor involved.

What does it take to be an investment banker?

- **Grades:** You need the best grades in both undergraduate and graduate schools.
- **Leadership:** You must show leadership in sports, campus government, or other extracurricular activity at college.
- **Balance:** You must show strong skills in both analytic and quantitative subjects.
- **Interpersonal skills:** You must show that you can work with people and can sell.
- **Ambition:** Investment banking is an all-consuming job. It requires you to abandon your social life. It is not a place for anyone

who wants a family and quality time with their friends.

- **Stamina:** Eighty-hour work weeks are common in investment banking. You never know when you will be asked to fly across the country on a moment's notice and arrive ready to go to work. One newly arrived analyst worked nine months without a day off and claims he loved every minute of it.
- **The Right Personality:** Each firm has its own personality, and yours should match it.

Lawyer

Lawyers interpret laws for the benefit of their clients, individuals or businesses.

Banks and financial services businesses, in particular, are governed by a multitude of federal and state laws and regulations. Corporate lawyers make sure that the companies they work for comply with these laws and regulations, and they represent the company when legal actions are brought. They review and prepare major contracts involving the corporation, negotiate with other lawyers, and review leases for the company's property.

As advocates, lawyers represent their companies in criminal and civil trials. As advisors, they provide advice about the company's legal rights and obligations and suggest courses of action.

Corporate lawyers often specialize in one area of law such as tax law, international law, civil rights law, securities law, or insurance law. Some act as trial lawyers and represent the company in court.

Corporate lawyers often work long hours, especially in the banking and finance areas, where many documents must be filed for securities offerings, mergers, or divestitures.

Corporate lawyers handle most of the legal work required by the company, but time-consuming or highly technical matters may be given to outside law firms.

To practice law in a state, the lawyer must be licensed or admitted to the state's bar association. Most states require lawyers to pass a difficult exam, and many also require them to take a separate ethics examination.

Lawyers need a bachelor's degree. Undergraduate programs should emphasize communications, logic, public speaking, and general humanities courses. As with most jobs, familiarity with computers is helpful.

Lawyers are also required to complete at least three additional years of legal study and graduate from a law school approved by the American Bar Association. Many approved law schools offer night classes for people who must work full-time.

Competition for law schools is vigorous, especially for the more prestigious schools. The first year and a half is spent studying basic law courses such as property law, procedures, and legal writing. The student then chooses a specialty such as tax law or corporate law, and concentrates his or her study in that area.

Law firms often offer summer clerkships that provide opportunities to obtain references and jobs after graduation. Some specialties, such as tax, require the lawyer to obtain an advanced degree.

Few corporations have the resources to train new attorneys. They prefer to hire attorneys who have had experience in private law firms.

Once the lawyer is practicing, the studying does not end. It is critical that a lawyer stays abreast of what is happening in his or her client's industry and in the laws that are affecting that industry.

Beginning corporate lawyers earn an average of $51,000 a year, but that quickly reaches six figures and continues to grow as the lawyer's tenure with his or her company increases.

Marketing

Marketing is matching products and services with buyers to make a profit for the company. It sounds like a much easier job than it is. Often, marketing, advertising, and public relations employees work together to sell the company's products or services.

Marketing

Marketing professionals determine the demand for the company's products and services, identify potential customers, put together a pricing strategy to maximize market share and profits, monitor trends, identify new products and services, and oversee their development.

Sales Professional

Sales professionals make sure that the products and services are sold and sales goals are met. They set up training programs to make sure salespeople understand what they are selling and how the products and services meet potential customers' needs. They determine the sales potential of new products and services and keep track of what customers want so that they can recommend new products or services, or suggest that older ones be eliminated.

Advertising Professional

These workers usually represent the company with outside ad agencies. They decide what kind of advertising is needed and where it will produce the best results. They are often directly involved in all creative aspects of a company's ads.

Public Relations Professional

PR people use publicity to promote the company's products and services. They clarify or justify the company's decisions and points of view to make sure that the company's image is what it should be in the eyes of the public.

Marketing jobs usually require people to put in long hours, including evening and weekend work. Most professionals work under tight print or video production deadlines, and last minute changes or problems are common. Many of the jobs require extensive traveling.

A bachelor's degree is necessary, and a liberal arts background is preferred. Most employees also need to take classes in accounting, marketing, economics, finance, and statistics, among others. Strong written and oral communications skills are a basic requirement.

The U.S. Department of Labor estimates that these jobs will grow faster than many other jobs through the end of the century because of increased competition for customers. Annual salaries range from under $30,000 to more than $250,000, and many companies pay bonuses that can increase earnings by 10 percent or more.

Research Analyst

Research analysts study securities—usually stocks—and make recommendations on what to buy and sell. Their advice is used by a wide range of other professionals in banking and finance, such as institutional and retail brokers, investment bankers, and trust and portfolio managers.

Analysts follow certain industries and companies within those industries, trying to learn everything they can about them. Most analysts are experts in twenty or thirty stocks in one or two industries. Some analysts may be experts in more than 100 stocks.

Some of the things the analyst must learn about each company are its history, management, products, markets, financing, past earnings, and future earnings potential. To do this, they must understand accounting rules and study all kinds of financial reports and statements about the company.

Analysts take all the information they gather and write research reports, recommending buy, sell, or hold positions on every stock for which they are responsible. The analyst gives his or her recommendations to the company's brokers or, sometimes, directly to the company's customers.

Analysts have tremendous power in a brokerage firm. A good analyst whose recommendations result in profits for customers and the company becomes a hero. When a respected analyst changes his or her mind, the price of a stock can rise or fall based solely on the analyst's recommendation to buy or sell. Analysts also spend time traveling, visiting the companies they follow and attending conventions and trade shows.

Once a year, *Institutional Investor* magazine surveys institutional clients on who they think are the best analysts and publishes the results.

Top analysts can earn $500,000 a year. Starting salaries can be as high as $65,000 a year. Analysts also earn bonuses.

The Financial Analysts' Federation provides a designation of Chartered Financial Analyst to analysts who complete a series of rigorous essay examinations. To pass the exams, applicants need an extensive knowledge of accounting, economics, securities, and many other areas. But the CFA designation is almost as important as an MBA, and in many firms it is the preferred designation for analysts.

Secretary or Administrative Assistant

Behind every successful businessperson is a good secretary, sometimes also called an administrative assistant. Administrative assistants keep their bosses functioning efficiently. They are the primary communicators of information as they perform a wide variety of important duties.

Administrative assistants make appointments for their bosses, answer callers' questions, maintain files, complete forms, take dictation, type correspondence and documents, schedule and coordinate meetings, make travel arrangements, and maintain information on computers. Administrative assistants must know how to use spreadsheets, database management, and graphics programs. Administrative skills are in demand in almost every industry and profession.

Employers want people who have at least a high school diploma and know basic office and software skills. Good time-management and organizational skills are helpful.

Typing, spelling, and a good grasp of grammar and punctuation are a few of the requirements to be a secretary. Shorthand or familiarity with dictation equipment is a plus, as is the ability to use word processing equipment and computers.

Good interpersonal skills are definitely an asset, since the secretary works closely with people at all levels—both inside and outside the company.

Experienced administrators can apply for the designation of Certified Professional Secretary (CPS) given by the Institute for Certifying Secretaries, a part of Professional Secretaries International. Candidates attain the designation by passing a series of examinations, and it is a mark of professional excellence.

Experienced administrators can become executive secretaries to the partners or more senior members of a firm.

Secretaries must be able to adapt to change and learn how to use new office equipment. As more and more office jobs are being automated, the secretary must develop a full range of skills in order to keep up with office technology. In addition, many secretaries work for more than one person in the company, and must be willing and able to juggle conflicting assignments and priorities.

Annual salaries range from $28,000 to $39,000 a year, and can go much higher for executive secretaries who work for senior executives.

Trader

If you have seen pictures of the floor of an exchange such as the Pacific Stock Exchange, you have seen what bedlam looks like. People rushing around, shouting, waving hands and papers at each other. The action revolves around the pits, depressions in the floor where the traders buy and sell. It's hard to believe that all the frantic gestures and cryptic shouted messages mean something, but they do.

Traders buy and sell all kinds of things—securities, options, commodities—for their clients or firms. They match buyers and sellers, often using their own or their firm's money to close a deal. Fortunes are made and lost in seconds.

Every trader develops his or her own style of money management. To counteract the extremes of Wall Street, however, many traders will also hold fixed-income securities, or money that retains its value if the market dips. Fixed-income securities can take many forms, but some of the most popular include corporate bonds, agency securities, and asset-backed securities. Other traders focus on equities as secure investments.

Many traders first experience the market by working for a public pension fund, a bank trust department, or a mutual fund department.

Traders have the fastest-paced jobs in banking and finance. As one experienced trader says, you have to master "the essential trader's trick of doing at least four things at once. Usually, talking to a client on the phone while writing out a trading ticket, keeping a watchful eye on the Dow-Jones tape, and listening to the calls of other traders in the room."

Jobs on the floor are represented by the color of the jacket worn. Pages, runners, messengers, and squads wear light blue. Reporters wear navy blue, and supervisors wear green. Those in street clothes are managers, directors, officers, and employees of other firms, such as:

Commission brokers, who buy and sell securities for their firm's customers.

Independent floor brokers, who are private entrepreneurs buying and selling for their own clients.

Registered competitive market makers, who trade either for their own account or their firm's account.

Exchange officials, who accommodate all orders to keep the market moving, or liquid.

Competitive traders, who trade for their own accounts.

Stock specialists, who act as the focus of the market for specific stocks assigned to them.

Agents, who bring buyers and sellers together.

The major form of communication in the jumble is the famous Dow-Jones ticker tape. Once a strip of paper, it is now electronic. Each stock is identified by one, two, or three letters. Below and to the right of the symbol are the number of shares traded and the price. In addition, news bulletins play across an electronic news board overlooking the pit.

Investment bankers trade thousands of shares of stock a day that represent millions of dollars. In some firms, salespeople serve as middle persons between the bank's customers and its traders who execute the transactions. In other firms, the trader also acts as a salesperson.

Commercial bankers also maintain trading operations, mostly for the use of their institutional customers, but trading is dominated by the investment banks.

Traders cannot afford to leave the floor for a moment. They can lose millions of dollars by missing an opportunity to buy or sell a stock. There are no power lunches or even long bathroom breaks for traders during business hours—9:30 AM to 4:00 PM Eastern Standard Time.

Traders must be able to think fast, concentrate in the midst of chaos, and make split-second decisions. These skills are more important than a college degree. They also have to understand odds and risks and feel at ease with numbers.

Arbitrage is a form of trading. It involves simultaneously buying a contract in one market and selling it in another market for a price that is higher than the buying price. Profit is instantaneous. Arbitrage is becoming more and more common in mergers and acquisitions, when one company buys another company.

Business Week magazine described an arbitrageur in its August 13, 1984, issue as "a trader who thrives on rumors, buying up shares quickly on hints of a raider's interest in the hope of reselling them to anyone willing to pay a premium for control of a company."The movie *Wall Street* was the story of an arbitrageur, the infamous Gordon Gekko, played by Michael Douglas.

One out of three traders burn out in a year. They can't take the stress or the pressure, or they can't make enough trades to earn an income. Salaries range from $31,400 to $103,000 and depend on performance.

Interview: Marty Cunningham
senior vice president, Nasdaq and Institutional Trading, Schwab Capital Markets, LP

Q: What got you into this business?
A: In my last year of high school, I got a job as a broker messenger at the wholesale brokerage where my cousin worked. In college, I worked in the "back office" at a brokerage house, reconciling the books and records. After college, I completed a five-year apprenticeship and was promoted to trader in 1987—the month of the big stock market crash. What an education! I saw despair and panic. I was energized, but I didn't want to run, I wanted to stay. Time and time again, the industry lives through downturns and profits.
Q: What are your key responsibilities?
A: I am responsible for Schwab's market-making subsidiary and for building its institutional franchise on the trading side.
Q: What qualities make someone a good trader?
A: First, he or she has to have an appetite for risk— that's what got me into the business. Second, the person has to be flexible. Some traders develop opinions and then are unwilling or unable to shift gears when market conditions change. Third, traders have to think quickly

on their feet. Fourth, traders must resist the temptation to be too analytical when trying to figure out why stocks go up and down.

Q: What's the difference between a good trader and a great trader?

A: Of course, it's important to be knowledgeable about the industry, to know what risks to take, and to be able to roll with the punches, but really successful traders have developed a certain intuition, a "feel" for the business. Great traders just have that ability, and it's not something that one learns from reading books.

Q: How should someone proceed who wants to pursue a career as a trader?

A: A degree is still not a prerequisite, but we do want people who are well-rounded. Some companies like Schwab have one-, two-, or three-year programs that will give selected employees hands-on experience in a variety of areas, such as back-office analytical work, sales, international, research, and technology. That's an excellent way to learn about the company and decide where you might best fit.

Trust Officer and Portfolio Manager

The officers in a bank's trust department manage billions of dollars in assets for other people and organizations. Trust officers manage all kinds of assets, including real estate, securities, money, and even artwork. Some are also portfolio managers. These assets are placed in trust with the bank, which manages them according to the client's wishes.

Some of the trust accounts that a department may manage are money for wealthy people, endowments for schools, pension and profit-sharing money for companies, and retirement funds.

Sometimes a person makes arrangements to have the trust department manage his or her estate after death. This often happens if the person's heirs are minors, for example.

"Employees in the trust area may have a legal background in order to interpret and follow legal instructions in trust agreements," says Wells Fargo's David Skolnik. "They also need good people skills since they often work closely with multigenerational families."

The portfolio manager decides what securities should be bought for each portfolio for which he or she is responsible. To do this, the portfolio manager relies on his or her own experience and on information gleaned from research analysts, each of whom follows one or more industries.

Portfolio managers are also responsible to an investment committee. All transactions must meet the requirements set down by the committee, which decides if certain investments are acceptable for its portfolios.

As in most areas of banking and finance, competition is fierce and in getting more so. Trust and portfolio managers who earn the best returns on customers' investments retain their existing clients and gain new ones through recommendations.

"These employees need to understand the U.S. and global economies, how they work, and how they are interconnected," says Wells Fargo's Skolnik. "They must be able to read a company's balance sheet and research a company. It's a lot more than just knowing and picking stocks."

Some companies hire employees with BA degrees, but more and more companies require a graduate degree. Experience in other areas of securities or research analysis is usually required to be a portfolio manager, so it is not an entry-level job. More entry-level jobs are administrative assistant or portfolio assistant positions that allow employees to advance to more senior jobs.

Annual salaries range from the low twenties for entry-level jobs to more than six figures for senior managers.

Insider Information

"The laws regulating our markets are a product of the New Deal era. To me, their concepts are as indelible as the Constitution. They have weathered challenge after challenge, decade after decade, and are every bit as relevant and effective today as they were the day they were written. Companies offering their shares— whether off a Web site or through a paper prospectus—still have to disclose what they are selling and why. Brokers—whether traditional or online—still have the same obligations to their customers. And fraud—whether perpetrated over the Internet, on the phone, or in person—is still fraud."

—Arthur Levitt, chairman, U.S. Securities and Exchange Commission

Employees in banking and finance often have access to secret information. It may be confidential information about a client or customer. Or, employees may learn information about a company or customer before that information is released to the general public.

This kind of information is called insider information. If an employee reveals insider information to anyone, his or her career, along with the reputation of his or her bank or financial institution, can be damaged. It is also against the law to use insider information for personal gain.

The following are some kinds of insider information to which employees in banking and finance have access:

- The sale or purchase of assets before the transactions are made public.
- Possible mergers and acquisitions
- Accounting reports about a client or another company that are unavailable to the general public
- Discussions of customer transactions
- Letters or other documents that describe or mention deals

For example, let's say you are working on the financial statements of XYX company because your client, PQR company, wants to buy it. That is insider information. You cannot discuss what you know with anyone outside the company. You may not even be able to discuss it with some people inside the company. For instance, you could not tell a broker or trader about the pending acquisition. If you did and the broker or trader bought stock in XYX company, all involved would be breaking the law regarding using insider information for gain.

The key rule followed by all employees of banks and financial institutions is: Protect information.

Insider Trading: Not Worth the Risk

Trading that occurs because of inside information is called insider trading. This became a hot topic in the news in the 1980s, when several high-profile cases were exposed. Ivan Boesky became a household name in 1986 when he was arrested for insider trading and pled guilty to all charges. Boesky was fined $100 million, spent three years in prison, and was forever banned from trading on the New York Stock Exchange.

Insider trading did not cease to be a problem even after that well-publicized case. The Securities and Exchange Commission, which enforces insider-trading regulations, reports that insider trading never really tapered off. In 1998, the SEC investigated 350 insider-trading allegations, up from 45 in 1994 and 1995. SEC officials say that the high number of mergers in the current economy accounts for much of the insider trading that occurs.

In an unusual case in 1996, the former chief financial officer of Intuit, Inc. told his wife that the software company was going to be purchased by Microsoft. The wife shared the information with her son and daughter. Based on this information, the son, daughter, and three of their friends traded Intuit stock. The SEC filed a federal civil suit against the five who had traded, as well as against the wife who passed on the information. All six settled the suit by paying $472,000, without admitting or denying wrongdoing.

Today, insider trading is not just committed by financiers and corporate CEOs. The average investor may find himself or herself at risk. According to an article in the *Los Angeles Times*, an advertising executive had confidential information that a client company was about to acquire another company. The SEC alleged that the executive bought shares of the company being acquired before the announcement of the merger and then sold the shares after the merger. The SEC investigated, and, while the executive neither admitted nor denied wrongdoing, the SEC required the executive to pay more than $200,000 in penalties and to forfeit the proceeds from the transaction.

Getting the Job
You Want

"The most exciting part of my job is working with exciting people who are changing the world of technology. I am running a business where I am the boss and am responsible for setting my own schedule and being in a job where I can make as much money as I am able with no limitation."

**—Derek B. Fowler,
senior vice president, Investments
Salomon Smith Barney**

Different jobs in banking and finance require different qualifications. A high school diploma will get you in the door for some jobs, such as the position of broker or trader. Other entry-level positions that do not require a college degree are bank teller, bookkeeper, accounting clerk, data entry keyer, file clerk, secretary, and word processor. For most of these jobs, you will need a thorough grounding in mathematics, an attention to detail, and a familiarity with computers. Be sure to take math classes in high school, as well as accounting, bookkeeping, economics, business, and computer classes if they are offered. If your school has a business club, you should consider joining.

If you are interested in being a broker or trader, you will also need a basic understanding of the way the stock market works.

As in most other fields, if you want to advance up the corporate ladder, you will eventually need a bachelor's degree. A bachelor's degree is also a minimum requirement for many of the entry-level jobs discussed in this book.

You need not study only business or accounting in college. Bankers and brokers come from all kinds of backgrounds—English literature, psychology, international relations, even art history. College undergraduates may want to concentrate on a major that shows they can think, analyze, and write. Many banks and financial companies prefer liberal arts majors who have strong communication and analytical skills, and who like to work with people.

Many of the higher-paying jobs in banking and finance demand a graduate degree or master's in business administration, which means that you must make long-range plans if you want one of these positions. The superstar jobs on Wall Street, in banking—or anywhere else, for that matter—require great qualifications and, in many cases, connections. You'll need high grades from the best schools for the really prestigious jobs, and you'll also need to get plenty of work experience under your belt.

For all of these jobs, the job hunt begins right now.

Do Your Homework

To start planning for a job in this competitive field, do your research early. Read books on investments and the companies involved in banking and finance. Some interesting ones are listed in the For More Information section of this book.

Read newspapers such as *The Wall Street Journal* and the *New York Times*. Read magazines such as *Forbes*, *Fortune*, and *Business Week* to gain an understanding of the industry. Consumer magazines such as *Money*, *Kiplinger's*, and *Online Investor* will teach you how consumers view financial and banking services and products, and teach you about the customers served by the financial services industry.

Watch television programs and visit Web sites that discuss investments and the economy.

The Internet is also a good source of information. In addition to the home pages of individual companies, some online service providers offer Web sites containing their own financial reports on many companies, as do some banks and financial services companies. Many banks and brokerages have their own home pages where you can learn more about the business. Online financial forums and discussion groups are other good places to find out about the worlds of banking and finance. You can also call companies directly and ask to be sent copies of their annual reports. If a company is publicly traded, you can get a copy of the proxy report, which gives biographical and compensation information on the company's officers. Many companies will send you corporate histories or recruitment materials.

Even though you might not be actively seeking full-time employment until after you graduate from college, you can still talk to campus recruiters to help you narrow your choice of jobs and companies. The college campus career center or placement office has information on the fields in which you are interested. Learn as much as you can about the differences between the jobs and the companies.

Alumni from your college will probably be glad to speak with you and answer questions. But don't call on these people until you have done your homework: Read all you can on your own. Always send a cover letter explaining who you are, what you want, and that you will call in a week or two with your questions. This type of research is called an informational interview.

Informational Interviews

Prepare a list of questions beforehand so you will remember what you want to cover. The more specific your questions are, the better. This will improve the cooperation you will receive. The questions below should give you an idea of what to ask during an informational interview.

How did you become interested in banking and finance? How did you get your first job? How should a person who is interested in banking or finance prepare for a career? What do you like most about your position? What do you like least about your profession? What kind of challenges or problems do you have to deal with in your job? What sorts of skills do you need to succeed in your job? What is your typical day like?

Don't take more than thirty minutes of the person's time. At the end of each call, ask the person if he or she can recommend someone else for you to talk to. Send thank-you notes to everyone you interview.

Networking

Networking is one of the best ways to hear about potential jobs. Networking doesn't have to be an elaborate process. To start, make a list of all your friends. Then expand your network to include everyone else with whom you have even a passing acquaintance: relatives, your friends' parents, classmates, teachers, professors, counselors, local shopkeepers and business people, your parents' friends, the banker at your local branch, the people who gave you informational interviews, and anyone else you know.

Write each person's name down on a separate index card or make space for them in a computer file. Then, begin contacting everyone in your network. Ask them specific questions: Do they know of any jobs that you might be interested in? How about at their company? Can they introduce you to someone who might give you more information? As in the informational interviews, don't forget to thank them afterward. Keep track of when you speak to each person and what they told you. A simple way is to write it directly on the index card or add it to the computer file. These steps help you build a network that will prove valuable not only when you are ready for full-time employment, but when you want a summer job at one of the firms in which you are interested.

Internships

Internships are very valuable. Part-time and summer jobs provide experience-based learning. You have a chance to "reality test" how you feel or fit in a specific job situation. You get first-hand experience and the ability to see how your education fits into the real world. You also develop a track record of competence, getting things done, building self-confidence, and garnering recommendations for future employers.

To prepare for an internship, work with someone on the college career placement staff to explore areas of interest, kinds of activities, relationships, roles, and what excites you. Most banks and financial institutions offer internship programs through local colleges and universities.

Preparing a Résumé

Now that you've researched possible banking careers and know which kind of job interests you most, it's time to put that knowledge to good use. The first step in landing an interview is crafting the perfect résumé.

A résumé is basically an outline of what you've done and where you want to go. Think of your résumé as a sophisticated sales tool designed to sell the thing you know best: Yourself. If you have never done one before, take some time to sit down and think about what you would like to say about yourself. Feel free to draw up several different drafts and experiment with the best way to package your skills. Whatever you choose to say about yourself, you should include the following information on your résumé:

- Your name, address, and telephone number.

- Education. Include where you went to high school or college, your grade point average, what degrees you received and when, and any academic honors. If you are attending or have graduated from college, it is not necessary to include your high school history.

- Work experience. Use the names and locations (city and state) of companies that you have worked for, and a short list of your responsibilities at each job. This can include part-time or temporary work, internships, and any volunteer work that you have done (although some people choose to include volunteer work in a separate category).

- Membership in clubs or organizations. Mention any varsity or intramural sports, especially if you were captain or team leader, as well as participation in other activities.

- Military history, if applicable.

- Skills. Be sure to list any computer, communication, and foreign language skills that you have. Show proof that you can write, analyze, and think on your feet.

When preparing your résumé, keep these tips in mind:

- **Keep it short and to the point**. Use the fewest words possible to say what you want to say. Your résumé should fit on one page; use two pages only if absolutely necessary.

- **Make it easy to read**. Organize the different sections so that key points grab the reader's attention. It's okay to use italicized and bold type for emphasis, but use each sparingly.

- **Be dynamic**. Use action verbs: directed, analyzed, initiated, launched, etc.

- **Proofread your résumé.** Read your résumé until you know that it is perfect. Any typos or grammatical errors could cost you an interview. Have someone else proof it, too, just to be sure.

People with many years of work experience sometimes list their employment history in a functional rather than a chronological format. This means that they group their jobs and related experience under different categories, such as supervisory experience, manual labor experience, or customer service experience.

Most people who are in the early stages of their career organize their skills and experiences in a chronological format. To follow this format, list your experience beginning with your most recent job first and work your way backward. The following sample résumé was written in a chronological format.

Jenny McGrath
143 Valencia Street
San Francisco, CA 94116
(415) 555-8396

Education
San Francisco State University, San Francisco, CA
Bachelor of Arts expected May 2000.
Major: Economics. **Minor:** Russian Literature. **GPA:** 3.45

Work Experience
Bank Teller, Wells Fargo Bank, San Francisco, CA
June 1998–Present
Process withdrawals and deposits; wire money; issue traveler's checks, foreign currency, savings bonds, and certificates of deposit; balance cash against transactions. Won the Employee of the Year Award for the San Bruno Avenue Branch in 1999.

Volunteer Team Leader, University Outreach Project
September 1997–Present
Supervise ten overnight camping trips a year for groups of inner-city girls ages eight to fourteen.

Waitress, The Lobster Pot, Half Moon Bay, CA
June 1997–August 1997
Full-time Server.

Skills
Excellent math, writing, and customer service skills. Familiar with Microsoft Word and WordPerfect word-processing software. Fluent in Russian and Spanish.

References available upon request.

You can also include the following if you wish:

• **Career objective.** This is the name of the job that you are applying for, such as assistant branch manager or junior accountant.

• **Relevant courses.** High school or college classes you have taken.

• **Personal data.** Birth date and marital status, hobbies, other interests.

What can you put in your résumé that will especially impress an interviewer who has seen and heard it all?

• **A knowledge of accounting.** You don't have to major in it—and you probably shouldn't unless you want to be an accountant—but you need a working knowledge of accounting principles. It also shows that you are serious about your intent to pursue a job in banking or finance.

• **Work experience in finance or banking.** Choose summer jobs in the banking or financial services industry. Most branch offices of brokerage firms use college summer help. Some offer paid and unpaid internships. Listing one or more of these jobs will give you an advantage. Many banks hire college students as part-time tellers or clerical employees.

- **Work experience in sales.** If you can't land a job in the finance or banking areas, sell something. Many of the jobs in banking and finance require sales experience.

- **Memberships.** Companies want both leaders and team players. Make sure your résumé shows that you are one or the other (or both).

- **Advanced studies.** Try to take advanced courses in economics, math, composition, finance, and computer science. These courses are especially important if you major in a nonbusiness subject, such as history, English, or psychology.

Cover Letters

A cover letter should accompany your résumé and emphasize why you are qualified for the job. Cover letters are short, just a few paragraphs at most. The first paragraph usually includes the title of the job you are applying for and where you saw the job opening (or who told you about the job). Cover letters are a good place to put all that research you did earlier to good use. Mention any facts that you may have read or researched about the company. Make sure to print your cover letter on the same kind of paper and in the same style as your résumé. Also, carefully proof the letter before you send it out. Have someone else proof it, too. A sample cover letter follows:

143 Valencia Street
San Francisco, CA 94116
(415) 555-8396

April 28, 2000

Mr. Fred Nagasaki, Vice President
United Savings Bank
San Francisco, CA 94313

Dear Mr. Nagasaki:

I am writing to you to apply for the position of personal trust assistant as advertised in the *San Francisco Chronicle* on April 27. My résumé is enclosed for your review.

I am currently finishing my senior year at San Francisco State University. My major courses have included micro and macro economic theory, international business, and computer-based information systems.

For two years I have worked full-time during summers as a bank teller for Wells Fargo. In this time, I have gained a thorough grounding in basic bank procedures. I have also become skilled at dealing with all types of customers and meeting their needs quickly and efficiently.

I believe that I have what it takes to make an excellent assistant in the field of personal trust. My background in banking, combined with my knowledge of the field of economics, would be an asset to your trust department at Union Savings Bank. I would welcome a chance to meet with you in person. I look forward to hearing from you.

Sincerely,
Jenny McGrath

References

In addition to your résumé, you should also have a list of at least three people who know you fairly well and who have agreed to provide a reference for you. These can be former employers, high school teachers, college professors, or anyone except relatives. Although you will not be listing them on your résumé, you can expect to be asked for this list of references during an interview. Print the list of references on the same kind of paper on which your résumé is printed. Ask people if you can use them for a reference before giving their names to a prospective employer. Make sure that the people you choose have a positive opinion of you and will give you an excellent reference. For each reference, list the person's name, job title, company name and address, and telephone number.

The Interview

You've sent out your résumés and cover letters. Now companies are beginning to contact you for interviews. Don't panic! Think of the interview as a fact-finding mission, not a test. It's up to you to figure out if you would be comfortable working at the company. Go ahead and ask questions of your own. What are the possibilities for career advancement? What would your typical day be like? Why did the interviewer choose to work for that particular company? What are appropriate goals for the person in the job in question to set?

Spend some time before the interview thinking of questions that you might be asked and the answers you would give. On the day of the interview, dress conservatively. Bankers dress to blend in, not to stand out, so wear a conservative business suit to your interview. Bring along an extra copy or two of your résumé and cover letter.

Relax and try to remain positive. Eventually, you will get a job. And then the real work begins!

Interview: Alex Armstrong, CFP
Armstrong, MacIntyre & Severns, Inc.
Derek Fowler, SVP, Investments
Salomon Smith Barney

Q: Describe your career path.
Armstrong: I was a stockbroker before getting my CFP designation, the first license like it in Washington, DC.

People will buy stocks from a twenty-five-year-old, but it is unlikely that they will feel comfortable giving him or her their entire financial portfolio and asking for planning and investment advice. This is one field where age—maturity—is an advantage. People want to feel you know something about life before they trust you with all their money and their financial future.

Over my years as a stockbroker, many of my clients would ask me about wills, mortgages, and inheritances. I just knew about investments. I wanted to be better equipped to answer their questions. As I got older and more experienced, I knew I wanted to do more than just buy and trade stocks.
Fowler: I first worked as a stockbroker, which is basically a sales job. Then, I developed marketing strategies for new clients to help them improve their financial portfolios.
Q: What are your responsibilities?

Armstrong: There are three aspects to the CFP process: financial planning, working with clients, and investing.

To be involved in the planning side, you have to have a head for numbers; to be involved in the client side, you have to enjoy working with people and be empathetic to their concerns.

An individual comes in and fills out an eight-page questionnaire about how they spend money, what assets they have, etc. I review their responses, looking at individual factors such as their age, job history and income, the number of years to retirement, and their financial risk tolerance. I charge a fee (an hourly rate) to produce a financial plan, and meet with them to discuss it. I make adjustments based on our discussion and give them a copy. I also charge a fee for providing an ongoing review of their financial situation. That includes making revisions to their financial plan as needed (usually every three to four years), and providing them with financial counseling services. It's important to build relationships over time; I've had some clients for twenty or thirty years now.

Fowler: I am a relationship manager. I lead a diversified team of advisors to help high-net-worth executives (those with portfolios of $10 million or more), establish financial and estate planning programs for customers and their heirs. My team includes estate planners, attorneys, and tax accountants, among others. My particular job is very entrepreneurial, like running a small business. We bring in clients and manage their portfolios, outsourcing various services so we can keep our focus on the big picture.

In the world of high-net-worth marketing, we don't buy and sell stocks, we outsource that responsibility to third-party institutions. We concentrate on the macro issues and advise clients about financial strategies.

Q: What attributes are important?

Armstrong: The ability to manage stress, to easily shift from one subject to another as clients' needs change, and to delegate. A CFP also needs to have patience, sincere empathy, and strong organizational skills. One thing that makes the job interesting and challenging for me is that I need to shift gears based on the needs of each client. The market changes constantly, and the needs of every client are different.

I go to financial planning conferences, read financial magazines, and watch television programs such as *Wall Street Week*. I want to spot trends. If I see the same topic covered in several articles, I'll know a trend is developing.

Be well-read in your area of specialty. And, if you're not very well organized, you're finished. Most important, you have to be a good salesperson because your livelihood literally depends on it. I get zero salary; I make money through asset management revenues and by selling financial products. The company that I work for gets a percentage of what I sell, and I also get a percentage, or commission.

Fowler: If you want to be a relationship manager, it's not good to get caught up in the tactical aspects of the market—the everyday ups and downs. If that interests you, stick to research on the institutional side of the business, where you'll get involved in analyzing companies. That area of the financial services industry requires people with strong math skills.

I prefer business development and coordinating financial plans. In this side of the business, you have to

be careful not to overanalyze the market. More impor-
tant than having strong math skills, you have to have
strong sales skills and love working with people. It's the
more intuitive end of banking, whereas the research
area is much more analytical. Interestingly, the most suc-
cessful person I know on this end of the business was a
drama major in college.

Q: Do you see any trends developing?

Armstrong: There's a trend toward more specialization
now, just as there is in the medical profession. There is
so much information out there and things are so com-
plex, that being a generalist isn't as helpful as knowing
one segment very well. For example, a planner may
decide to work with single women, small business
owners, or generations within the same family.

I recently cowrote a book with a psychologist on
investment planning for widows. The book examines
how to deal with the grief that accompanies the loss of a
husband, and the change in a woman's financial situation
as a result of becoming widowed. It can be a very con-
fusing, frightening time for women, and I want to help
them avoid costly mistakes.

Also, more than 15 percent of financial planners are
women, and the number continues to grow.

Fowler: Wall Street brokerage houses and banks are
merging at a fast rate now. That means that we have
more resources at our disposal and can offer clients
more services under one roof.

If you're an old-world broker, just buying and selling
stocks, you're in serious trouble. Clients can buy and
trade stocks for themselves now, so why should they
pay someone else to do it? The industry is moving
toward offering fee-based asset management services,

rather than offering commissioned transaction services. Many of my clients like to do some online trading, so, as part of the added-value services I offer, I set them up so they can trade using a very small percentage of their portfolio. I charge them, say, 1 percent, which is much less than they would pay in commissions on each trade.

Q: What advice would you give someone interested in getting into the field?

Armstrong: You're not going to be successful as an independent without paying your dues first. I think it's good to get into an apprenticeship program. To begin, I'd suggest looking up the local chapter of a financial planning member association. Attend their meetings, network, and get informational interviews with CFPs. I'm too busy during business hours, but I do attend meetings and then I am happy to talk with people. That's also a good way to find out which companies have good apprenticeship programs.

Fowler: For someone just starting out, you can use age to your advantage. For instance, I'm thirty-one years old and I work in the high-tech industry. Many of my clients are of similar age and have similar interests. We speak the same language, so it's easy for me to relate to them, and they feel comfortable working with me.

Glossary

accountant   Specialist who prepares and analyzes the financial transactions of a business and may make recommendations for financial decisions.

accounting   Keeping track of financial records: how money flows into, through, and out of a business.

administration   Department of a company that provides support services, such as equipment requisition and personnel management.

American Stock Exchange (Amex)   Stocks of lesser-known companies are bought and sold on this exchange.

analyst   Specialist in a particular industry or several industries. The analyst researches everything available about his or her specialty, synthesizes that information, and makes recommendations about what stocks within that industry a company should buy and sell. Good analysts can forecast future industry trends.

annual report Statement of how a company has done financially in the past year.

appraiser Person who estimates the value of real estate or personal property.

arbitrage Taking advantage of price differences in securities or commodities traded on different exchanges, or between new and old securities of a single company. The arbitrageur takes opposing positions in the hope of turning a profit from temporary price differences.

assets Property owned by or owed to a company or person.

auditor Person who examines financial records to ensure their accuracy.

automated teller machine (ATM) Electronic banking machine that takes deposits and issues withdrawals.

average Measure of trends in stock prices.

banker Person who works in the banking industry.

bank operations Functions that support daily banking activities; also called back-room operations.

bear market Period during which stock prices go down.

benefit managers Professionals who design and administer benefits programs.

benefits Non-monetary compensation given to employees, such as health care, life insurance, and retirement plans.

bond Debt security. A company issues bonds to people and organizations that lend the company

money. The company pays either a set or a
fluctuating rate of interest to the bondholders and
promises to redeem the bonds at a future date.

bookkeeper Person who maintains financial
ledgers, or records.

broker Agent who buys and sells securities
for customers.

brokerage Company that offers financial and
investment services to individual and
institutional customers.

budget Written plan for handling income
and expenditures.

bull market Period during which stock prices
go up.

business administration Study of how businesses
are operated, business principles, and practices.

call Option to buy a security.

capital Goods or money used to generate income.

capital market Security market such as the bond or
stock market.

cash flow Movement of money into, through, and
out of an organization.

cash manager Controller of the flow of money.

certificate in management accounting (CMA)
Designation conferred by the National Association
of Accountants (NAA) to those who pass a series of
exams and meet certain standards.

certificate of accreditation in taxation Designation
conferred by the Accreditation Council for
Accountancy and Taxation of the National Society
of Public Accountants.

certificate of deposit Savings instrument deposited
for a specified period of time.

certified information systems auditor (CISA)
Designation conferred by the EDP Auditors
Association on candidates who complete five years
of experience in the field.

certified internal auditor (CIA) Designation
conferred by the Institute of Internal Auditors, Inc.,
on graduates of colleges and universities who have
two years of experience in the area and who pass a
four-part exam.

certified professional secretary Designation given
by the Institute for Certifying Secretaries, a part of
Professional Secretaries International. Candidates
must pass a series of exams to obtain the
designation.

certified public accountant (CPA) Licensed and
regulated accountant.

chartered financial analyst Designation conferred
by the Financial Analysts Federation on research
analysts who complete a series of exams.

check Authorization for a bank to draw money from
an account and pay it to the person or organization
to whom the check was written.

checking account On-demand deposit that can be
withdrawn by checks.

clearing agent Agency that provides capital and
office support and functions as a bank for traders.

clerk Employee who keeps track of records and files
and handles various pieces of office equipment,
such as typewriters, calculators, and computers.

cold call Call to a stranger by phone or in person to
try to sell him or her something.

collateral Something of value put up to secure
a loan.

commercial bank Bank that provides services to corporations and individuals.

commission Fee earned or amount charged for buying and selling something, such as stocks.

commodities Objects of commerce, such as crops, hogs, lumber, and gold, that are bought and sold.

Commodity Futures Trading Commission (CFTC) Federal agency that regulates commodity trading.

community bank Small bank, usually suburban or rural.

compensation Salary and monetary rewards, such as bonuses, given to employees.

compensation manager Executive who develops pay policies for a company.

compliance Actions of a company to meet government regulations and its own corporate standards.

computer operator Person who handles data by computer.

computer programmer Person who writes computer instructions in a computer language.

conglomerate Corporation made up of many different parts or companies.

controller Financial manager responsible for the accounting, audit, and budget departments of a company.

corporate money manager Specialist who manages a corporation's money, recommending and managing its investments.

corporate securities Stocks or bonds issued by a company to raise money.

credit Time given for payment for purchases.

credit union Cooperative association that offers

banking services such as savings accounts and loans to its members.

customer service representative   Employee who deals directly with customers, resolves customer problems, and makes sure that the customer receives good service.

data processing   Function that inputs and works with information on computers.

dealer   Person who acts as a principal. Dealers buy securities for their own accounts and then sell them to customers.

deposit   Money or valuables placed in a bank for safekeeping.

depositor   Person who puts money in a bank account.

deposit slip   Paper record of money placed in a bank account.

deregulation   Removal of government regulations from an industry.

discount brokerage   Company that offers financial and investment services at reduced commission fees.

dividend   Earnings on stocks; money or additional shares of stock paid to stockholders based on number of shares owned.

Dow-Jones average   Average of the prices of thirty outstanding industrial stocks listed on the NYSE.

Dow-Jones ticker tape   Electronic record of buys and sells of securities.

economics   Science of the production, distribution, and consumption of goods and services.

economist   Person who studies and applies the principles of economics.

electronic banking   Banking services provided by computer.

employee benefit plans   Insurance and savings plans offered by companies to employees and their families, such as life insurance, retirement plans, health care, vacations, and profit sharing.

Equal Employment Opportunity (EEO)   Hiring of people without regard to factors unrelated to the job, such as race, sex, or sexual preference.

equity   Stock that represents ownership in a company.

Federal Reserve System   Agency established in 1913 by the Federal Reserve Act to regulate banking.

finance   Science of managing money.

financial statements   Various presentations of a company's financial status that appear in its annual report.

floor   Trading area of a stock exchange.

foreign currency   Money issued by foreign governments.

futures contract   Agreement to buy or sell a commodity at a future date.

Garn-St. Germain Depository Institutions Act   Legislation passed in 1982 that allowed banks to offer new products and deregulated much of the industry.

Glass-Steagall Act   Legislation passed in 1933 that separated commercial banks and investment banks and prohibited commercial banks from underwriting corporate securities.

government bonds   Debt obligation issued by federal, state, or municipal government.

grievance   Complaint by a union employee against the company.

holding company   Nonoperating company that owns or has a controlling interest in the securities of other companies that do operate as businesses. For instance, BankAmerica Corporation is the holding company for Bank of America and Seafirst Corporation, among other companies. Seafirst Corporation, in turn, is a holding company for Seafirst Bank.

home banking   System that allows customers to make banking transactions with personal computers in their offices or homes.

home improvement loan   Loan made to upgrade a home using the home as collateral.

human resources department   Part of a company that establishes personnel policies and procedures.

individual retirement account (IRA)   Savings instrument that defers and reduces taxes on deposits.

inflation   Rise in prices and wages.

insiders   Directors, officers, and major securities holders of a corporation; usually they own more than 10 percent of the company.

insider trading   Buying or selling securities on the basis of information that has not been made public; a violation of federal law.

institution   Financial company that invests large amounts of money, such as an insurance company, a corporate pension fund, a mutual fund, or a trust department. Most of the money traded in the various securities markets comes from institutions.

institutional broker   Middle person between institutional investors and research analysts.

institutional investor   Organization having large amounts of money invested in securities.

insurance company   Business that sells protection against certain losses to individuals or corporations.

insured savings vehicle   Savings investment guaranteed by the government.

interest-bearing checking account   Checking account that pays interest on deposits.

interest rate   Amount of money paid to depositors or investors on their money or to lenders; usually a percentage of the principal.

internal auditor   Employee who audits a company's financial transactions and procedures.

investment bank   Bank that underwrites securities; it helps clients raise money through mergers and acquisitions, acting as a middleman between companies and investors.

investor   Person who commits money to an investment in the hope of earning more money.

job analyst   Person who compiles information on job duties.

license   Permission by authority to perform certain activities such as selling securities.

load   Sales charge imposed on investors in mutual funds.

loan   Money borrowed.

loan officer   Bank employee who makes decisions about lending money to customers.

management fee   Fee charged to investors by mutual funds for professional management.

margin   Customer's equity in securities purchased on credit from a broker.

marketing Matching products and services to customers to make a profit for the company.

market makers Traders who trade for their own accounts or for their firm's account when an exchange official orders them to do so.

McFadden Act Legislation passed in 1927 that forbade banks to open branches outside their home state.

merger Combination of two or more companies into one.

merger and acquisition Takeover of one company by another.

microfilm Documents maintained on film, not paper.

money market account High-quality, short-term instrument such as certificate of deposit, treasury bill, and commercial paper.

money market mutual fund Pool of a group of investors' money used to buy high-quality, short-term instruments.

money market securities Money market securities; short-term obligations of borrowers such as the U.S. Treasury, federal, state, and local governments, banks, and corporations.

mortgage Use of a home as collateral on a loan.

municipal bond Debt obligation to raise money.

mutual fund Pool of investors' money used to buy investments in larger amounts than would be possible for individual investors. The money is invested in a diversified list of securities chosen by the fund.

mutual savings bank Nonprofit business owned by its depositors.

National Association of Securities Dealers Automated Quotation System (NASDAQ) An inter-dealer market of more than 600 securities dealers; association of brokers and dealers in the over-the-counter market.

New York Stock Exchange (NYSE) The world's largest securities exchange, located at 11 Wall Street, with a trading floor the size of a football field. More than 2,000 stocks are listed on the so-called Big Board and are traded on the floor of the exchange daily.

NYSE index Average of all the stocks listed on the NYSE.

option Right to buy or sell a stock at a fixed price by a certain date.

personnel department Department of a company that handles human resources functions such as staffing, equal employment opportunity, training, compensation, and benefits.

pit Locations on the trading floor where commodities brokers and traders work.

portfolio Collection of securities held by an individual or institutional investor.

premium Price paid for an option.

printout Hard copy of computer data.

private bank Bank owned by private investors and offering limited services to a small group of wealthy investors.

private placement Securities transaction between two or more private parties without involvement of an exchange.

privileged information Confidential information communicated between two parties.

prospectus Document filed with the Securities and Exchange Commission when a company offers stock for sale.

publicly traded Bought or sold on an exchange.

public relations Use of ads and publicity to inform customers of the products and services the company has to offer.

put Option to sell a security.

recession Slowdown of the economy.

recruiter Employee who locates and hires qualified people for open positions.

registered representative Broker or account executive who has passed certain tests and met standards set by the NYSE, the NASD, or both.

research analyst See analyst.

retail bank Bank providing services to individuals.

retail broker Broker who advises individual investors on what investments to make to meet their goals.

retailer Business that sells goods to consumers for personal or household use.

retirement planning Planning for investments to provide a certain level of income at retirement.

safe deposit box Container placed in a bank safe for the storage of valuables.

sales manager Executive who supervises the sale of a company's products and services.

savings account Vehicle for investing money and receiving regular guaranteed interest payments.

savings and loan association Institution owned by depositors or stockholders that chiefly provides mortgages.

seat Membership on a stock exchange with the right to buy and sell securities on that exchange.

securities Stocks and bonds.

Securities and Exchange Commission (SEC) Federal agency established to regulate trading in securities.

selling group Group of investment banks and brokerages that agree to sell securities.

spread Difference between two prices; for instance, the difference between what an investment bank pays for an issue of stock and what it sells the stock for.

Standard & Poor's Indexes of 425 industrial stocks and 500 other stocks traded on the NYSE.

stock Share of ownership in a company.

stockbroker Person who buys and sells stock for individual investors.

stock exchange Place where a market for securities is made.

stockholder Person who owns shares of stock and has the right to vote on the election of the company's directors and other affairs.

syndicate Group of banks that agree to underwrite securities.

tax Money levied by a government authority on income, profits, property, etc.

tax shelter Investment having tax benefits.

time certificate of deposit Investment of a specific amount of money for a given period of time in order to earn a higher rate of interest.

trader Person who buys and sells stocks for profit, taking advantage of small price changes.

trust department   Department of a bank that manages assets for individuals or institutions.

trust fund   Investments held by one party, such as a bank, for the benefit of another party, such as a minor.

underwriting   Assuming the risk of insurance or agreeing to purchase an issue of a security for the purpose of selling it to the public.

wholesale banking   Commercial banking.

withdrawal   Taking money out of an account.

For More Information

American Bankers Association (ABA)
1120 Connecticut Avenue NW
Washington, DC 20036
(800) BANKERS
Web site: http://www.aba.com

American Institute of Banking (AIB)
1120 Connecticut Avenue NW
Washington, DC 20036
(202) 663-5429

American Economic Development
   Council (AEDC)
1030 Higgins Road, Suite 301
Park Ridge, IL 60068
(847) 692-9944
e-mail: aedc@aedc.org
Web site: http://www.aedc.org

American Financial Services Association
919 18th Street NW

Washington, DC 20006
(202) 296-5544
Web site: http://www.americanfinsvcs.org

American Institute of Certified Public Accountants
1211 Avenue of the Americas
New York, NY 10036-8775
(212) 596-6200
Web site: http://www.aicpa.org

American Stock Exchange
86 Trinity Place
New York, NY 10006
(212) 306-1000
Web site: http://www.amex.com

Bank Administration Institute
One North Franklin Street, Suite 1000
Chicago, IL 60606-3421
(800) 224-9889
Web site: http://www.bai.org

Certified Financial Planners Board
1700 Braodway, Suite 2100
Denver, CO 80290-2101
(888) CFP-MARK
Web site: http://www.cfp-board.org

Credit Union Executives Society
6410 Enterprise Lane, Suite 300
Madison, WI 53719-1145
(800) 252-2664, ext. 3400

e-mail: cues@cues.org
Web site: http://www.cues.org

Financial Women International
200 North Glebe Road, Suite 820
Arlington, VA 22203-3728
(703) 807-2007
e-mail: info@fwi.org
Web site: http://www.fwi.org

Institute of Management Accountants
10 Paragon Drive
Montvale, NJ 07645-1718
(800) 638-4427, ext. 265
Web site: http://www.imanet.org

New York Stock Exchange
11 Wall Street
New York, NY 10005
(212) 656-3000
Web site: http://www.nyse.com

U.S. Securities and Exchange Commission
Office of Investor Education and Assistance
450 Fifth Street, NW
Washington, DC 20549
(202) 942-7040
e-mail: help@sec.gov
Web site: http://www.sec.gov

Web Sites

http://www.bankjobs.com

http://www.banking.jobs-careers.com

http://www.bankingjobs.net

http://www.bankjobsearch.com

http://www.financialjobs.net

http://www.jobsinthemoney.com

http://www.nyse.com/jobs/jobs.html

For Further Reading

Aliber, Robert Z. *The New International Money Game.* 6th ed. Chicago: University of Chicago Press, 2000.

Chernow, Ron. *The House of Morgan: An American Banking Dynasty and the Rise of Modern Finance.* New York: Touchstone Books, 1991.

Downes, John. *Dictionary of Finance and Investment Terms.* 5th ed. New York: Barron's Educational Series, 1998.

Fitch, Thomas P. *Dictionary of Banking Terms.* 4th ed. New York: Barron's Educational Series, 2000.

German-Grapes, Joan. *The Teller's Handbook: Everything a Teller Needs to Know to Succeed.* 6th ed. New York: McGraw-Hill, 1997.

Gisler, Margaret, and Adrian A. Paradis. *Opportunities in Banking Careers.* Lincolnwood, IL: VGM Career Horizons, 2001.

Hunt, Christopher W., and Scott A. Scanlon. *Job Seekers' Guide to Wall Street Recruiters.* New York: John Wiley & Sons, 1998.

Kapadia, Anita, Chris Prior, and Tom Lott. *Vault.com Career Guide to Investment Banking.* 3rd ed. New York: Vault.com, 2000.

Lee, Helen, and Ying Liu, eds. *The Harvard Business School Guide to Careers in Finance, 2001 edition.* Boston: Harvard Business School Press, 2000.

Lewis, Michael. *Liar's Poker: Rising Through the Wreckage on Wall Street.* New York: Viking Penguin, 1990.

Liaw, K. Thomas. *The Business of Investment Banking.* New York: John Wiley & Sons, 1999.

Little, Jeffrey B., and Lucien Rhodes. *Understanding Wall Street.* 14th ed. New York: McGraw-Hill, 1997.

Maturi, Richard J. *Wall Street Words: From Annuities to Zero Coupon Bonds.* Rev. ed. Chicago: Probus Publishing Co., 1995.

Morgan, Bradley, and Joseph Palmisano, eds. *Business and Finance Career Directory.* Detroit: Visible Ink Press, 1993.

Morris, Kenneth, and Virginia B. Morris. *The Wall Street Journal Guide to Understanding Money and Investing.* New York: Simon & Schuster, 1999.

Naficy, Mariam. *The Fast Track: The Insider's Guide to Winning Jobs in Management Consulting, Investment Banking, and Securities Trading.* New York: Broadway Books, 1997.

Ring, Trudy. *Careers in Finance.* Lincolnwood, IL: VGM Career Horizons, 1999.

Ring, Trudy. *Choosing a Career in Banking and Finance.* New York: The Rosen Publishing Group, Inc., 1999.

Scott, David L. *How Wall Street Works.* New York: McGraw-Hill, 1999.

Tamarkin, Bob. *The Art of the Market.* New York: William Morrow, 2000.

Tamarkin, Bob. *The New Gatsbys: Fortunes and Misfortunes of Commodity Traders.* New York: William Morrow, 1985.

Woelfel, Charles J, ed. *Encyclopedia of Banking and Finance,* 10th ed. Chicago: Probus Publishing Co., 1994.

Index

A

accountant, 28–31, 55,
  57, 106
  CPA, 29, 30, 31
  duties of, 28–29
  education needed, 29, 30
  salary of, 31
  skills needed, 30–31
account executive, 24,
  35, 66
accounting, 16, 29, 34, 40,
  55, 57, 60, 61, 68, 71,
  72, 77, 78, 79, 89, 92,
  93, 101
Accreditation Council for
  Accountancy and
  Taxation, 30
Accredited in Accountancy
  (AA) designation, 30
Accredited Tax Advisor
  (ATA) designation, 30
Accredited Tax Preparer
  (ATP) designation, 30

advertising, 17, 76, 77, 91
American Bankers
  Association, 11
American Bar
  Association, 75
Ameritrade, 22
analyst/research analyst, 3,
  15, 22, 55, 65, 66, 67,
  68, 71–72, 73, 78–79,
  86, 87
  duties of, 78
  education needed, 79
  salary of, 79
  skills needed, 79
Anthes, Dr. William L., 57
appraiser, 45–46
apprenticeships, 109
arbitrage, 83
Armstrong, Alex, 105–109
assets, 85, 89, 106, 107, 108
ATM (automatic teller
  machine), 1, 9, 10–11,
  13, 32
  super-ATM, 10

attorney/lawyer, 15, 55, 57, 106
  duties of, 74, 75-76
  education needed, 75
  salary of, 76
  workday of, 75
auditor/auditing, 25, 28, 31
  duties of, 29
  education needed, 29, 30
  salary of, 31
  skills needed, 30-31

B
Bank Administration Institute, 30
BankAtlantic, 11
banking/finance
  administration, 16
  careers/employment in, 13, 14, 15-17
  future of, 10-13, 108
  history of, 5-7, 21
  how to get a job in, 94-105
  internationally, 14-15, 16, 44, 49
  new products/services and, 9-10, 17, 22, 52, 76-77
  paperless, 12
  skills/education needed for career in, 92-93
Bank of America, 40-41
Bankrate.com, 12
bank teller, 1, 2, 7, 12, 13, 31-33, 92, 100, 101, 103
  duties of, 31, 32
  education needed, 33
  opportunities for, 33
  salary of, 33
  skills needed, 31-32, 33
  workday of, 32, 33
benefits manager, 65

Boesky, Ivan, 90
bonds, 2, 7, 19, 24, 25, 26, 31, 35, 59, 66, 67, 68, 100
  corporate, 81
  government, 21, 59
bookkeeper/bookkeeping, 7, 16, 25, 34, 92, 93
bookkeeping and accounting clerks, 33-34
  duties of, 33-34
  education needed, 34
  salary of, 34
  skills needed, 34
  workday of, 34
Boston, 22
broker/stockbroker, 1, 10, 23, 24-25, 26-27, 34-41, 56, 61, 66, 78, 82, 88, 89, 92, 93, 105, 108
  duties of, 35, 36-37, 39
  education needed, 37, 40
  online, 22, 23, 88
  qualifications/skills needed, 35, 37-38, 40-41
  salary of, 36, 37, 38
brokerages, 2-3, 21, 22, 28, 38, 39, 53, 66, 69, 78, 84, 94, 101, 108
  discount, 10, 23, 37, 43
  employment in, 24-25
  Business Week magazine, 83-84, 94
buyouts, 2

C
cash manager, 54, 55
certificates of deposit (CDs), 31, 59, 100

Certified Financial Planner
(CFP) designation, 18,
60, 61, 63, 105, 106,
107, 109
Certified Information Systems
Auditor (CISA)
designation, 30
Certified Internal Auditor (CIA)
designation, 30
Certified Professional Secretary
(CPS) designation, 80
Charles Schwab, 5, 22, 84, 85
Chartered Financial Analyst
(CFA) designation, 79
checking account, 1, 2, 4, 8, 10,
11, 12, 26
checks, 7, 12, 31, 32
Chicago, 22, 47
Chicago Board of Trade, 47
Citibank, 15, 61
clerical employee/clerk, 13,
25, 34, 41–43, 50, 75,
92, 101
clerical supervisor/manager,
41–43
duties of, 41–42
education needed, 43
salary of, 43
skills needed, 42–43
workday of, 42
cold calls, 36–37, 44
college degrees, 18, 29, 31, 37,
43, 44, 45, 49, 50, 53, 55,
57, 60, 61, 62, 65, 67, 71,
72, 73, 75, 79, 87, 92,
93, 98
College for Financial Planning,
56, 57, 58, 60, 61

commercial banker/banking,
16, 22, 43–46, 69, 83
duties of, 43–44
salary of, 44
training programs, 44
commissions, earning, 22,
36, 37, 39, 60, 66, 71,
107, 108
commodities, 19, 22, 25, 26, 35,
46–48, 49, 81
exchange, 48
commodities trader, 46–49
duties of, 47–48
salary of, 48, 49
compensation manager, 64–65
competition, 2–3, 4, 5, 7, 9,
13, 14, 17, 19, 22, 23, 37,
44, 56, 67, 70, 75, 77,
86, 94
computers, 1, 9, 12, 12, 15, 16,
23, 24, 26, 29, 32, 33, 34,
37, 42, 46, 49–51, 53, 55,
65, 67, 72, 75, 79, 93, 96,
98, 102, 103
computer specialist, 13, 25,
49–51
education needed, 50, 51
opportunities in, 50
programmer, 15
salary of, 51
skills needed, 50
Congress, 6, 7, 9, 21
controller, 54, 55
cover letter, 95, 102–103,
104, 105
example of, 103
credit, 6, 43, 55
credit cards, 11, 12

Careers in Banking and Finance

credit unions, 13, 17–18
  education needed to work
    in, 18
Cunningham, Marty, 84–85
customer loyalty, 5, 13
customer service, 13, 18, 32,
    33, 43, 44, 51–52, 100
  salary of employees, 52
  skills needed to work in,
    51–52

D
debit (POS) cards, 12
Department of Labor (DOL),
    13, 24, 25, 29, 33, 53,
    56, 77
deposits, 7, 9, 10, 31, 32, 43
deregulation, 2, 5, 8–9, 22, 56
Dow-Jones ticker tape, 81,
    82–83

E
economist, 15, 52–53, 55
  duties of, 52–53
  education needed, 53
  opportunities for, 53
  salary of, 53
economy, effect on banking
    industry, 24, 25
electronic/online banking, 1, 9,
    10, 12, 13, 52
Equal Employment
    Opportunity (EEO)
    representative, 64
estate planning, 37, 58, 62, 106
estates, 13, 86
E*Trade, 22
eye scan, 1

F
Fidelity Investments, 5
file clerk, 53–54
  duties of, 54
  education needed, 54
  salary of, 54
financial adviser/consultant,
    23, 24, 25–26, 27, 35, 105
Financial Analysts' Federation, 79
financial manager, 54–56
  duties of, 55
  education needed, 55
  opportunities for, 55–56
  salary of, 56
  skills needed, 54
financial planner, 25, 56–63,
    106, 107, 108, 109
  duties of, 57, 58–60
  education needed, 57, 60, 61
  future of, 62–63
  opportunities for, 58
  salary of, 60
  skills needed, 57, 60, 61, 63
Forbes magazine, 94
foreign currency, 1, 10, 11, 16,
    31, 44, 100
Fortune magazine, 94
Fowler, Derek B., 92, 105–109
Frankenstein, George, 38–41
fraud, 29, 88
fund manager, 15
futures market, 24, 25, 47

G
Gannett News Service 70
Garn-St. Germain Depository
    Institutions Act, 9
Glass-Steagall Act, 7, 69

global village, 14
gold, 6, 26, 35
Gordon, Meryl, 70
greed, 20

H
human resources, careers in,
    17, 63-66
  duties of, 63-65
  education needed, 65
  salary of, 65-66

I
inflation, 56
informational interview,
    95-96, 109
Information Systems Audit and
    Control Association, 30
information technology, 16, 50
insider trading, 20, 71, 88-91
  history of, 90
Institute for Certifying
    Secretaries, 80
Institute of Certified Financial
    Planners, 60
Institute of Internal Auditors,
    Inc., 30
institutional broker, 39, 66-67,
    69, 78
  duties of, 66-67
  education needed, 67
  salary of, 67
Institutional Investor
    magazine, 79
insurance, 35, 37, 43, 55, 57, 58,
    59, 60, 62, 65, 74
insurance companies, 22, 33,
    35, 50, 53, 56, 57

interest, 6, 7, 8, 12, 67
Internet, 10, 11, 23, 27, 46,
    88, 94
internships, 31, 97, 98, 101
interviews, 97, 104-105
  informational interview,
    95-96, 109
Intuit, Inc, 90
investment banker/banking,
    20, 22, 24, 53, 67, 74,
    78, 83
  duties of, 67-68, 69-70
  education needed, 71, 72, 73
  salary of, 71-72, 73
  skills needed, 73-74
  team, 68-69
investments, 7, 8, 10, 12, 14, 16,
    17, 18, 20, 24, 25, 26, 27,
    29, 30, 35, 37, 39-40, 43,
    49, 55, 56, 57, 58, 60, 61,
    62, 66, 67, 86, 94, 105, 106

J
job analyst, 64

K
Kiplinger's magazine, 94

L
Lam, Catherine, 45-46
laws/regulations, government,
    2, 6, 7, 8, 9, 14, 17, 29,
    54, 55, 56, 65, 71, 74,
    88, 89
Levitt, Arthur, 88
licenses, 18, 30, 35, 57, 63,
    75, 105
loan officers, 43, 45, 55

loans, 1, 2, 4, 6, 7, 8, 9, 11, 14,
    15, 16, 26, 31, 37, 43, 45,
    46, 67
local banks, 1, 6, 17, 33, 96
Los Angeles Times, 91
Lufkin & Jenrette, 38

M
marketer/marketing, 13, 15,
    16-17, 25, 52, 53,
    76-77, 105
    education needed, 77
    opportunities for, 77
    salary of, 77
    skills needed, 77
McFadden Act of 1927, 14
mergers and acquisitions, 13,
    14, 17, 69, 70, 75, 83, 89,
    90, 91
Merrill Lynch, 5, 36
Microsoft, 90
Money magazine, 94
money manager, 9
money market accounts, 35
mutual funds, 8
Morgan Stanley Dean Witter,
    25, 72
mortgages, 8, 26, 35, 105
mutual funds, 8, 22, 25, 35, 59,
    61, 66, 81

N
Nasdaq, 50
National Association of Colleges
    and Employers, 31
National Association of
    Securities Dealers
    (NASD), 18, 24, 35, 57

National Bank Acts of 1863 and
    1864, 6
networking, 96, 109
new business group, 44
New York, 21, 22, 38
New York Stock Exchange
    (NYSE), 21, 35, 90
New York Times, 94

O
Oh, Sue, 25-27
Online Investor magazine, 94
online trading, 22, 25, 37, 109
options, 19, 47, 48, 59, 81
    call option, 47
    put option, 47

P
Pacific Stock Exchange, 81
partnerships, 4
pension funds, 16, 81, 86
pit, the, 48-49, 81
portfolio manager, 78,
    85-87, 106
    duties of, 86
    education needed, 87
    salary of, 87
    skills needed, 86-87
Professional Secretaries
    International, 80
profit sharing, 86
program manager, 18
public relations, 16-17, 76, 77

R
real estate, 7, 70, 85
record keeping, 16
recruiters, 64

refinancing, 26
research analyst, 3, 15, 22, 55,
    65, 66, 67, 68, 71-72, 73,
    78-79, 86, 87
    duties of, 78
    education needed, 79
    salary of, 79
    skills needed, 79
résumé, 97-102, 104, 105
    example of, 100
retail broker, 35
retirement account/fund, 10,
    35, 57, 58, 65, 66, 86
retirement planning, 25, 26, 56,
    57, 62
Roberts, Rosanne, 17-18

S
safe deposit box, 5
sales, 13, 15, 17, 18, 24, 25-26,
    37, 38, 40, 70, 76-77, 83,
    85, 102, 105, 107, 108
Salomon Smith Barney, 92, 105
Sanwa Bank, 45
savings account, 2, 4, 10, 11
secretary/administrative
    assistant, 39, 49, 72,
    79-80, 87, 92
    duties of, 79
    education needed, 80
    opportunities for, 80
    salary of, 80
    skills needed, 79, 80
securities, 7, 10, 13, 17, 21,
    24-25, 35, 37, 49, 54, 55,
    57, 58, 66, 68, 69, 71, 74,
    75, 78, 79, 81, 82, 85, 86, 87
    fixed income, 81

Securities and Exchange
    Commission (SEC), 29, 57,
    88, 90, 91
selling group, 69
silver, 6, 26, 35
Skolnik, David, 4, 37, 86
smart cards, 9, 10, 11
spread, 8, 47, 69
stock market, 7, 24, 29, 93
    crashes of, 7, 84
stocks, 2, 7, 10, 19, 23, 24, 25,
    26, 35, 39, 40, 56, 59, 65,
    66, 67, 68, 78, 82, 83, 87,
    89, 105, 106, 108
    buying/selling/trading
        online, 1, 22, 23-24,
        25, 27, 37, 109
Summers, Donald, 17
surcharges, 12
syndicate, 68

T
taxes/taxation, 28, 29, 30, 52,
    57, 58, 59, 62, 74, 75, 106
tax shelters, 35
technology, effect of new, 1-2,
    9, 10-13, 15, 23-24, 25,
    46, 51, 67, 92
trader, 24, 25, 40, 48, 49, 71,
    81-85, 89, 92, 93
    colors of jackets worn on
        stock exchange floor, 82
    duties of, 81, 82, 83
    education needed, 85
    salary of, 84
    skills needed, 83, 84-85
training managers, 65
transfers, 11, 12, 16

traveler's checks, 11, 31, 32, 100
treasurer/treasury, 29, 54
trust banking, 16, 81
trust funds, 57, 66
trust manager, 78
trust officer, 13, 85–87
    duties of, 85–86
    education needed, 87
    salary of, 87
    skills needed, 86–87

U
unions, 42, 63-64

W
Wall Street, 19-27, 37, 70, 71,
        81, 93, 108
    downside of, 20
    history of, 21
    jobs on, 19, 22, 24-25
    location of, 21, 22
    salaries of, 20
    technology and, 23-24
Wall Street (movie), 20, 84
Wall Street Journal, The, 94
"Wall Street Week"
        (TV show), 107
Wells Fargo, 4, 37, 86, 100, 103
Wholesale banking, 43

Z
Zarb, Frank G., 24

About the Author
Patricia Haddock owns a communications consulting business in San Francisco. She has written and produced a wide range of corporate communications, including brochures, newsletters, and speeches. Her clients include major banks, insurance companies, and entrepreneurs.

In addition to corporate communications, Ms. Haddock has sold ten books and more than 400 print and Web publications. She specializes in business, self-help, and creativity subjects and also teaches and lectures on writing and business subjects. Before becoming a full-time consultant, Ms. Haddock worked as a communications officer and manager for a major California bank. She is a member of the American Society of Journalists and Authors, the Authors Guild, and the Society of Children's Book Writers and Illustrators.

Acknowledgements
I want to say thanks to several people who took the time to help make this book more interesting: Editor and friend Heidi Garfield. My sister, Bev, who always believes. And lastly, Connie, a good friend gone too soon.

Series Design
Danielle Goldblatt

Layout
Nelson Sa